# The Education Center, Inc.'s

# Creative Crafts For Year-Round Fun
## Grades K–6

**Edited and compiled by:**
Jennifer Overend

**Edited by:**
Lynn B. Coble
Betsy Seale

**Illustrated by:**
Jennifer T. Bennett
Pam Crane
Teresa Davidson
Susan Hodnett
Rebecca Saunders
Barry Slate

**Cover designed by:**
Terri Anderson Lawson

**About This Book:** *Creative Crafts For Year-Round Fun* is a collection of arts-and-crafts projects tested and submitted by subscribers of *The Mailbox®* magazines. This book contains arts-and-crafts projects for fall, winter, spring, academic themes, and gifts, as well as a generous collection of projects for any time of the year. You'll find that most of the materials needed are readily available and that the instructions are easy to follow. Children in grades K–6 will be artistically inspired year-round. So let the fun begin!

**www.themailbox.com**

©1993 by THE EDUCATION CENTER, INC.
**All rights reserved.**
ISBN# 1-56234-092-1

**Manufactured in the United States**

# Table Of Contents

*Dear Parent,*

*For our upcoming art projects, we will be needing the supplies indicated below. If you are able to donate any of these items, please send the materials to school with your child. We appreciate your help!*

____ egg cartons
____ empty plastic milk jugs
____ cotton balls
____ ribbon
____ fabric scraps
____ buttons
____ pipe cleaners
____ sandpaper
____ baby food jars
____ wrapping paper
____ tubes from paper towels or toilet tissue
____ plastic drinking straws
____ discarded magazines or catalogs
____ clean Styrofoam meat trays
____ newspapers
____ wallpaper samples
____ yarn
____ sponges

____ glitter
____ paper plates
____ Popsicle sticks
____ empty plastic liter bottles
____ aluminum foil
____ Styrofoam packing pieces
____ empty coffee cans
____ discarded tennis balls
____ metal coat hangers
____ metal bottle caps
____ fabric trims (lace, ricrac, etc.)
____ plastic produce bags
____ empty cardboard salt containers
____ Styrofoam packing pieces
____ black or white plastic garbage bags
____ discarded socks
____ empty plastic margarine containers
____ paper lunch bags
____ plastic six-pack rings

Other: _____

_____

*Thank you!*

©The Education Center, Inc.

**Note To Teacher:** Before duplicating, check the items you need, add any other item(s) not on the list, and sign your name. Send this home with students at the beginning of the year or any time supplies are needed.

3

# Fall Picture

### Materials for one picture:

5" x 8" white paper
thin brown paint
paintbrush
plastic drinking straw (cut in half)
1" squares of tissue paper (yellow, orange, red,
   brown, green)
glue
6" x 9" brown construction paper

**Steps:**

1. Position the white paper vertically. Using the paintbrush, place a few drops of brown paint at the base of the paper; then blow through the straw piece, making the paint spread upward to form tree branches. Allow the paint to dry.

2. One at a time, crush assorted colors of tissue-paper squares and glue them onto the painted branches for autumn leaves.

3. Attach the completed picture to a background of brown construction paper.

Arrange the pictures as shown on a wall or bulletin board entitled "Falling Down."

*Beth Jones—Grs. 1 & 2, General Vanier School,
Fort Erie, Ontario, Canada*

# Fabulous Fall Fashions

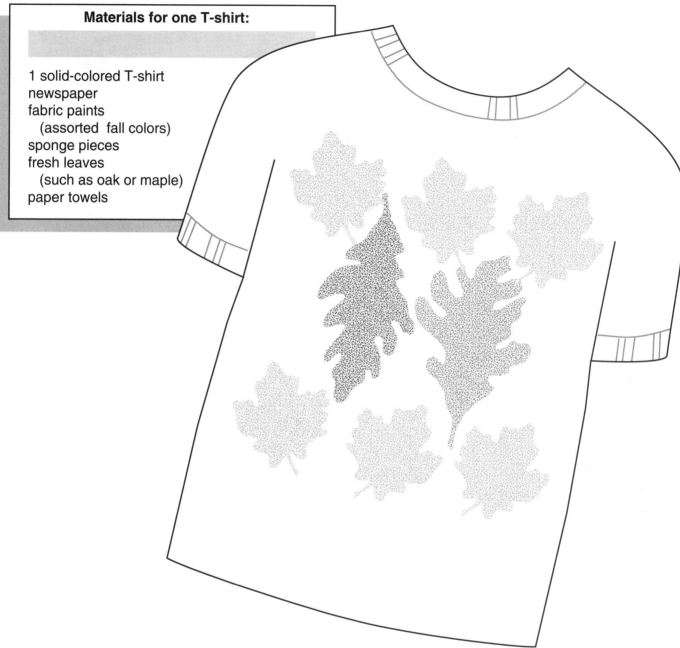

**Materials for one T-shirt:**

1 solid-colored T-shirt
newspaper
fabric paints
   (assorted  fall colors)
sponge pieces
fresh leaves
   (such as oak or maple)
paper towels

**Steps:**

1. Insert a double layer of newspaper inside the shirt.
   Lay the shirt flat on a tabletop.
2. Using a piece of sponge, lightly apply fabric paint to the veined side of a leaf. (More than one color may be used on a leaf.)
3. Lay the painted side of the leaf onto the shirt. Press down on the leaf with a paper towel.
4. Carefully lift the paper towel and the leaf from the shirt.
5. Repeat steps 2–4 to add the desired number of leaves to the shirt.
6. Follow the directions on the fabric paints for drying time.

Your students will enjoy wearing these colorful T-shirts to welcome the fall season.

*Carol Komperda—Gr. K, Albany Avenue School,*
*North Massapequa, NY*

# Leaf Rubbings

**Materials for one project:**

**leaf pattern on page 7**

8 ½" x 11" white paper (lightweight)
crayons
fresh leaves
scissors
9" x 12" colored construction paper
pencil
glue

Step 1

Step 3

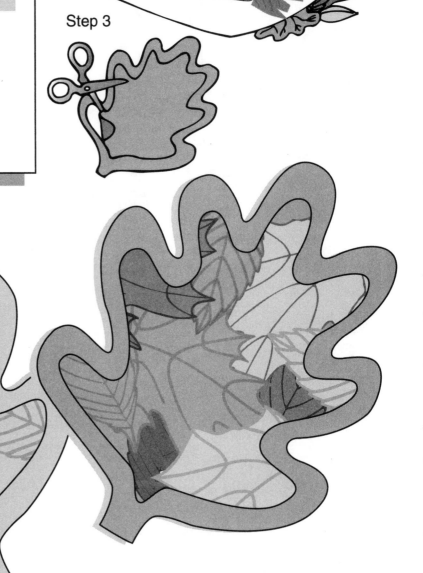

**Steps:**

1. Spread out several leaves and place the white paper on top of them. Using the sides of various colors of crayons, rub gently on the paper to make a leaf rubbing. Continue making leaf rubbings until the surface of the paper is covered. (Step 1)
2. Turn the paper over. Using the pattern on page 7, trace along its outer edges only. Cut on the resulting outline.

3. Using the same pattern, trace along both the pattern's inner and outer edges on construction paper. Cut on the resulting outlines to make a leaf frame. (Step 3)
4. Glue the frame atop the leaf rubbing, aligning the edges.

These leaves look especially nice when displayed in a window, allowing light to filter through them.

*Ana L. Wilson—Gr. 3, Ames School, Riverside, IL*

Use with "Leaf Rubbings" on page 6.

**Pattern**

**leaf frame**

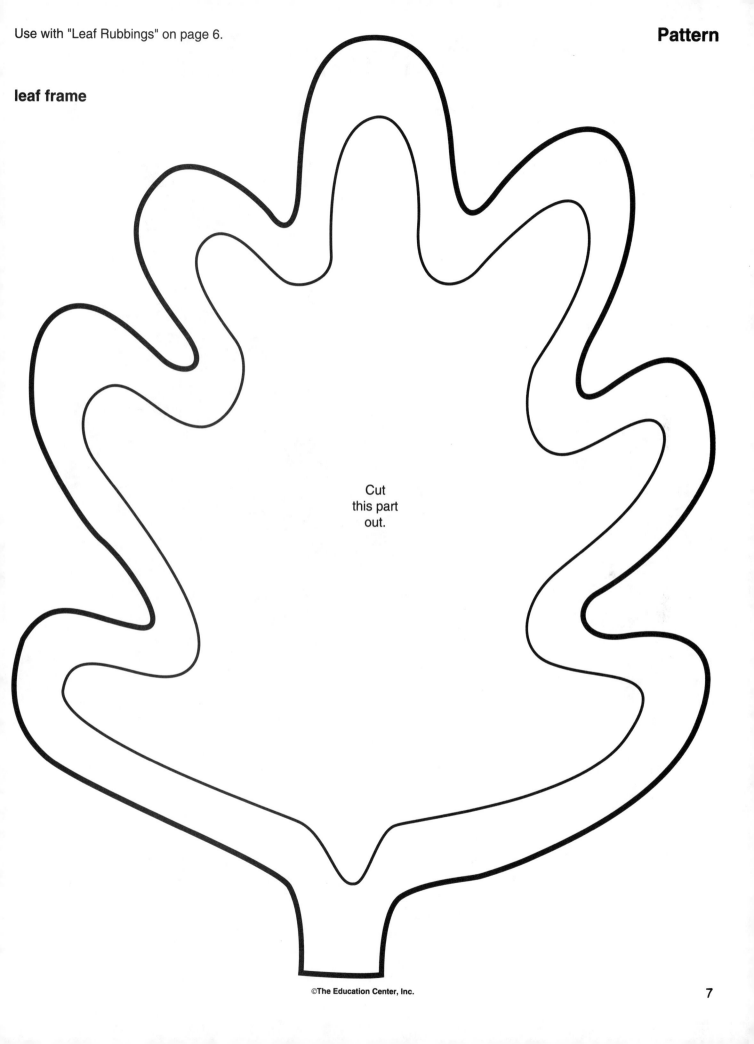

Cut
this part
out.

# Lovely Autumn Leaves

**Materials:**

**leaf patterns on page 9**

9" x 12" white construction paper
watercolor paints
paint brushes
water
scissors
glue
9" x 12" colored construction paper

**Steps:**

1. Duplicate the patterns on page 9 onto white construction paper.
2. On the blank side of the paper, brush autumn shades of watercolors over the entire page. Be sure to use enough water so that the colors blend into one another.
3. After the paints are dry, turn the paper over and cut on the leaf outlines.
4. Glue the leaves—painted sides up—onto colored construction paper, or staple them around a bulletin board for a festive fall border.

*Barbara H. Allison—Gr. 2, Tierrasanta Elementary School, San Diego, CA*

# Columbus Day Ships

**Materials for one ship:**

**sail patterns on page 11**

2 single-serving milk cartons (washed)
scissors                              glue
stapler
tempera paint
dishwashing liquid
paintbrush
white construction paper
crayons or markers
pipe cleaner

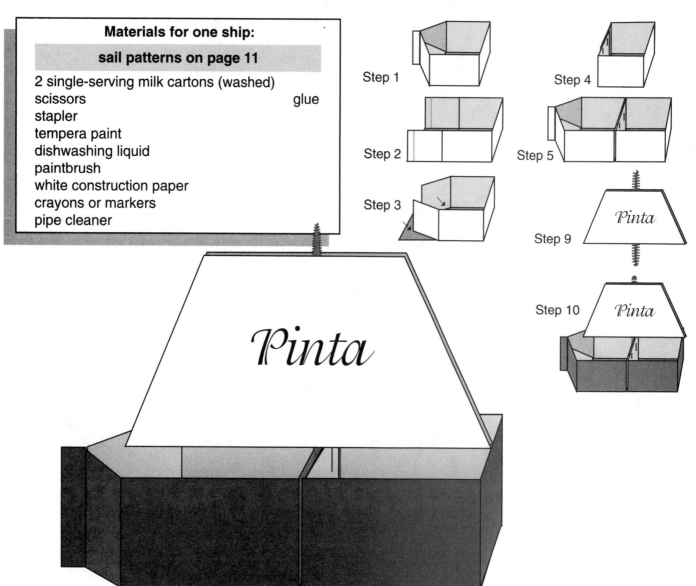

Step 1

Step 2

Step 3

Step 4

Step 5

Step 9    *Pinta*

Step 10    *Pinta*

*Pinta*

**Steps:**

1. Cut out the side of one milk carton and staple the end of the carton closed (Step 1).
2. Open the second milk carton and cut out one side (Step 2).
3. Cut two slits along the remaining natural folds of the second milk carton to form three flaps (Step 3).
4. Fold in the flaps and staple them together to make a rectangular box (Step 4).
5. Staple the two milk cartons together to form the body of the ship (Step 5).
6. Paint the ship with a mixture of tempera paint and a few drops of dishwashing liquid. (Dishwashing liquid prevents the paint from beading up on the milk cartons' surface.) Allow the paint to dry.

7. Duplicate or trace the sail patterns on page 11 onto white construction paper. Cut out the resulting outlines.
8. Using crayons or markers, write the name of one of Columbus's ships (Niña, Pinta, or Santa María) on one of the sails.
9. Place one end of the pipe cleaner between the two sails; then glue the sails together, aligning the edges (Step 9).
10. To attach the sail to the ship, insert the opposite end of the pipe cleaner between the two milk cartons. If necessary, staple the pipe cleaner in place. (Step 10)

*Jane Burk—Gr. 4, Sargent School, Monte Vista, CO*

**sail patterns**

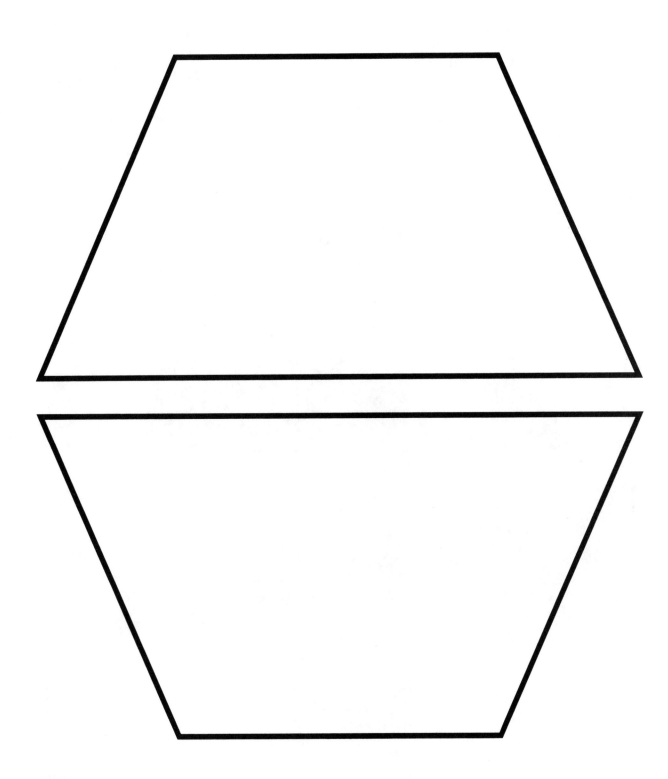

# Jack-O'-Leafy

**Materials for one project:**

**pumpkin and leaf patterns on page 13**

construction paper (orange, brown, yellow,
  green, black)
glue
scissors
pencil

**Steps:**

1. Trace around the patterns on page 13 and cut out one orange pumpkin, four brown leaves, two yellow leaves, and one green leaf.

2. Using black construction paper, cut out and glue jack-o'-lantern facial features to the pumpkin outline.

3. Glue the two yellow leaves to the pumpkin for arms.

4. For each leg, glue two brown leaves together and attach the leg to the pumpkin.

5. Glue the green leaf atop the pumpkin's head for a hat.

*Chris Irick—Gr. 2, St. Rose Of Lima, Great Bend, KS*

Use with "Jack-O'-Leafy" on page 12.

Patte

**pumpkin**

leaf

13

# Haunted House

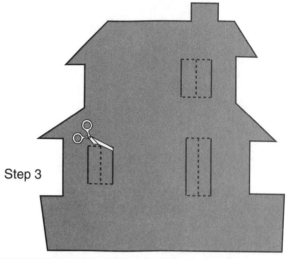

Step 3

**Materials:**

9" x 12" construction paper (assorted colors)
scissors
markers (black and other colors)
crayons
glue
Styrofoam packing pieces

## Steps:

1. Cut a house shape from construction paper.
2. On the house draw one door and two windows.
3. Cut along the top and bottom edges of the door and windows; then cut down the middle and fold back along the lines so that the flaps fold open (Step 3).
4. Glue the house onto a piece of 9" x 12" construction paper. (Do not glue the flaps of the windows and doors.)
5. Color a Halloween scene around the house using markers and crayons. Draw seasonal creatures inside the flaps of the door and windows.
6. Glue several Styrofoam packing pieces around the house for ghosts. Draw faces on the ghosts with a black marker.

*Karen Kuwik—Gr. 1, Truman Elementary, Lackawanna, NY*

14

# Halloween Spider

## Materials for one spider:

used tennis ball
6" length of black ribbon
  (or elastic)
1 package of black Rit
  dye (for all tennis balls)
newspaper
4 black pipe cleaners
hot glue gun

2 small orange
  pom-poms (for
  eyeballs)
2 tiny black pom-
  poms (for pupils)
school glue
scissors

*This project needs advance preparation by the teacher or a parent volunteer. It would also be helpful to enlist the help of a parent volunteer for the use of the hot glue gun.*

Step 1

Step 5

Step 7

Step 8

## Steps:
*(Steps 1–5 should be done by the teacher prior to this art project.)*

1. Use a saw to cut off the bottom of each tennis ball (about the size of a quarter). (Step 1)
2. Poke a hole in the top of each tennis ball. (You may want to enlist the help of a parent volunteer who could saw off the bottom of each ball and drill a hole in the top of each one at home.)
3. Mix the black dye according to the directions on the package. Soak the tennis balls in the dye overnight.
4. Set the tennis balls on newspaper to dry completely.
5. Using a paper clip or scissor point, push the end of the ribbon through the hole in the top of each tennis ball. Pull the ribbon through the bottom of the ball to make a knot; then pull the ribbon back through the top until the knot holds it in place (Step 5).

*(Steps 6–10 are to be completed by the student with the help of a parent volunteer.)*

6. Cut each of four pipe cleaners in half to make eight spider legs.
7. Bend the end of each pipe cleaner about a half-inch. Place the bent end of each pipe cleaner inside the hole in the bottom of the tennis ball. (Step 7)
8. Have a parent volunteer glue the pipe cleaners in place using a hot glue gun (Step 8).
9. When the glue hardens, bend the legs into the desired positions.
10. Glue the orange pom-pom eyes in place on the spider; then attach a tiny black pom-pom to each eye.

Sherri Nock—Gr. 3, Jupiter Farms Community School, Jupiter, FL

# Halloween Pumpkin

## Materials for one pumpkin:

used tennis ball
1 package of orange Rit dye
newspaper
1/2 of a green pipe cleaner
6" piece of narrow green ribbon
hot glue gun
2" square of black felt          school glue
scissors                               2 imitation leaves

*This project needs advance preparation by the teacher or a parent volunteer. It would also be helpful to enlist the help of a parent volunteer for the use of the hot glue gun.*

Step 1

Step 7

## Steps:

*(Steps 1–4 should be done by the teacher prior to this art project.)*

1. Using a saw, cut off the bottom of each tennis ball (Step 1).
2. Poke a hole in the top of each tennis ball. (You may want to enlist the help of a parent who could saw off the bottom of each ball and drill a hole in the top of each one at home.)
3. Mix the orange dye according to the directions on the package. Soak the tennis balls in the dye overnight.
4. Place the tennis balls on newspaper to dry.

*(Steps 5–9 should be completed by the student with the help of a parent volunteer.)*

5. Wrap one end of the ribbon around the end of the pipe cleaner and poke them into the hole in the top of the tennis ball.
6. Have a parent volunteer put a dab of hot glue around the hole to secure the ribbon and pipe cleaner in place.
7. Twist the pipe cleaner around the ribbon to give the pumpkin a curly stem (Step 7).
8. From felt, cut the pumpkin's eyes, nose, and mouth. Glue the felt pieces to the pumpkin with school glue.
9. Glue the leaves to the bottom of the pumpkin for a finishing touch.

*Sherri Nock—Gr. 3, Jupiter Farms Community School, Jupiter, FL*

# Halloween Creatures

**Step 3**

**Step 4**

**Steps:**

1. Using the pattern on page 18, trace or duplicate two bats onto black construction paper. Cut on the resulting outlines.
2. Use a white crayon to draw the face and the outline of the bat's body on one of the cutouts. Add details with other colors of crayons.
3. Cut ¼-inch-wide streamers in the plastic square, stopping each cut approximately one inch from the end as shown in Step 3.
4. Glue the uncut portion of the plastic between the two bat cutouts, allowing the streamers to hang from the bottom of the bat (Step 4).
5. Using a hole puncher, punch a hole near the top of the bat. Attach a length of yarn for suspending it.

Follow the same steps to make a ghost, using the ghost pattern on page 19, white construction paper, a black crayon for outlining, and a six-inch square cut from a white plastic trash bag.

*Paula Kear—Gr. 4, St. Mary's School, Ellis, KS*

Use with "Halloween Creatures" on page 17.

**bat**

Use with "Halloween Creatures" on page 17.

ghost

# Dodecahedron Jack-O'-Lantern

**Materials:**

pattern below
orange construction paper
scissors
glue (Use a thick craft glue for faster drying.)
green and black construction-paper scraps

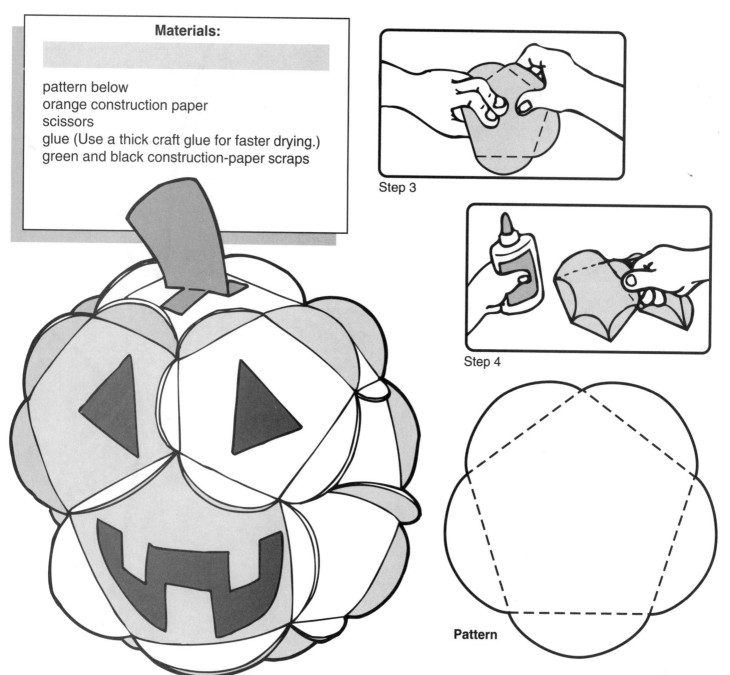

Step 3

Step 4

**Pattern**

**Steps:**

1. Duplicate the pattern shown 12 times onto orange construction paper.
2. Cut out the resulting outlines.
3. Position each cutout so that the dotted lines are faceup. Then fold each tab away from you on the dotted line as shown in Step 3.
4. Begin gluing the tabs of the outlines to one another. All of the tabs should face outward. (Step 4)
5. Continue gluing the tabs together until a dodecahedron (12-sided shape) is formed.
6. From green and black construction paper, cut a pumpkin stem, eyes, and a mouth. Glue the pieces to the pumpkin.

This project is a nice addition to a unit about geometric shapes.

*Lisa Scheffel—Gr. 5, Bobier Elementary School, Vista, CA*

# Shapely Scarecrow

**Materials for one scarecrow:**

construction paper (assorted colors)
scissors
1 sheet of white 12" x 18" construction paper
glue
straw (used to pack cartons)
markers

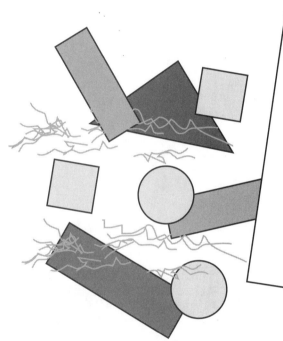

**Steps:**

1. Cut shapes from assorted colors of construction paper. You will need one large circle, four small circles, one large triangle, one small square, one large square, and four long, thin rectangles. (You may want to provide patterns for these six different shapes and have students trace the patterns as indicated and cut out their tracings.)
2. Glue the large square in the center of the 12" x 18" construction paper for the scarecrow's body.
3. Glue the large circle at the top of the body for a head. Attach a large triangle hat to the scarecrow's head.
4. Glue arms and legs in place using the long, thin rectangles. Attach the small circles to the ends of the rectangles for hands and feet.
5. Attach the small square to the body of the scarecrow for a pocket.
6. Complete the scarecrow by drawing facial features with markers and gluing on pieces of straw as shown.

*Kathleen Miller—Gr. K, Our Lady Of Mount Carmel, Tenafly, NJ*

# Magnificent Mayflower

### Materials for one ship:

9" x 12" brown construction paper
scissors
2 drinking straws
stapler
hole puncher
3 squares of 4" x 4" white construction paper

Step 2

Step 3

Step 4    Cut.    Cut.

Step 5    ← straw

Step 7
Cut. →    ← Cut.

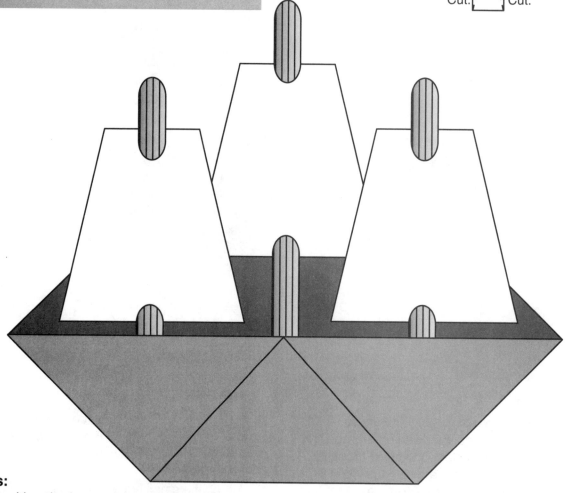

## Steps:

1. Position the brown paper horizontally.
2. Bring in the bottom corners to meet each other and crease as shown (Step 2).
3. Bring the bottom point up to meet these corners and crease again (Step 3).
4. Cut off the excess construction paper as shown (Step 4).
5. Position the bottom half-inch of one straw under the three intersecting points in the middle of the paper. Staple it in place. (Step 5)
6. Cut the remaining straw in half. Staple each half in the pocket on opposite ends of the ship.
7. Trim the white squares as shown to make sails (Step 7).
8. Using a hole puncher, punch a hole at the top and bottom of each sail.
9. Slide the straws through the holes in the sails.

*Sally A. Wolfe—Gr. 1, Washington Elementary School, Allentown, PA*

# Textured Turkey

Patterns

**Materials for one turkey:**

paper plate
orange, red, and yellow tempera paint
sponges
red, orange, and brown construction paper
scissors
head, foot, and wattle patterns below
dry cereal (various kinds)
glue
1 large wiggle eye                                   pencil

head

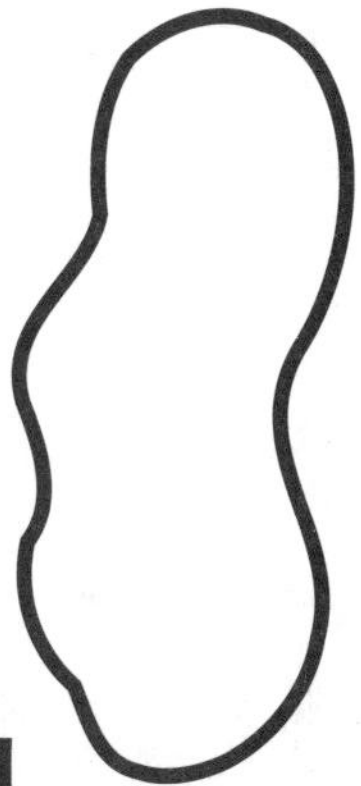

wattle

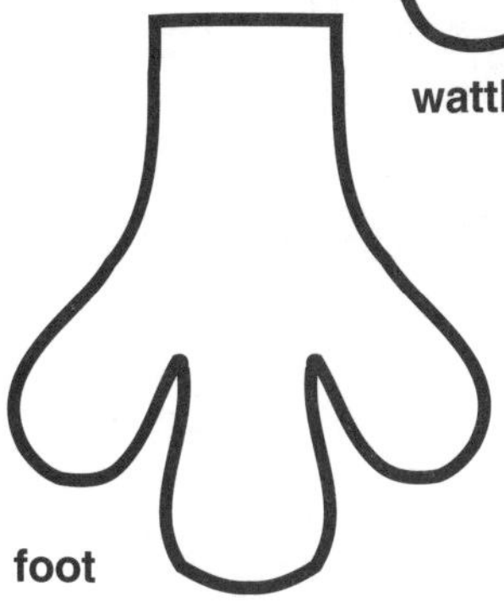

foot

**Steps:**

1. Sponge paint the paper plate with orange, red, and yellow paint. Let it dry.
2. Use the patterns shown to trace two turkey feet on orange construction paper and a wattle on red construction paper. Trace a turkey head onto brown construction paper. Cut out the resulting outlines.
3. Glue the feet to the back of the paper plate near the bottom.
4. Glue the head, wattle, and wiggle eye in the center of the plate as shown.
5. Glue various types of dry cereal to the paper plate to add a textured look.

*Jenny Eickhorst, Fort Wayne, IN*

# Turkey Napkin Holder

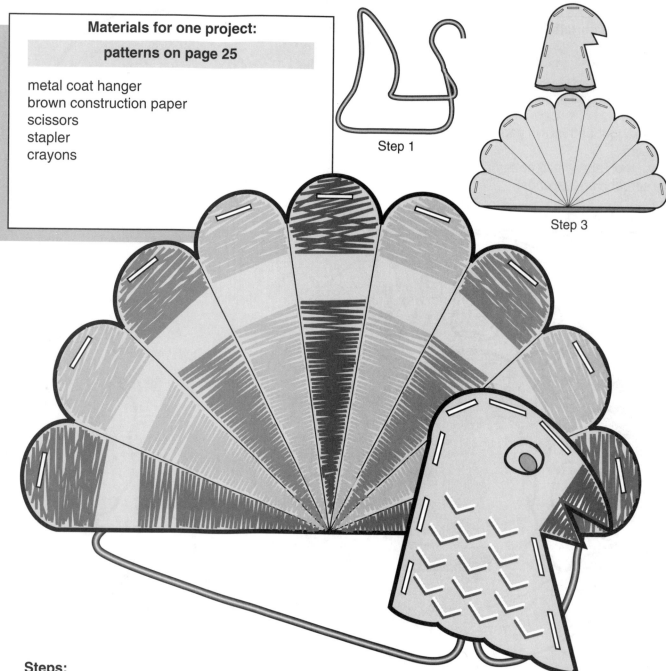

**Materials for one project:**

**patterns on page 25**

metal coat hanger
brown construction paper
scissors
stapler
crayons

Step 1

Step 3

**Steps:**

1. Bend the coat hanger into the position shown in Step 1.
2. Using the patterns shown and on page 25, trace two turkey heads and two tails onto brown construction paper. Cut on the resulting outlines.
3. Stack each pair of heads and tails, aligning the edges. Staple along the edges, leaving the bottom edges of the head and tail open. (Step 3)
4. Color both sides of the head and tail.
5. Slide the hooked end of the hanger into the open edge of the turkey head. Then slide the broad end of the hanger into the turkey tail.
6. Place napkins between the head and the tail, and use the napkin holder for a decorative centerpiece.

*Jeanne Ringer—Gr. 3, Washington Elementary, Piqua, OH*

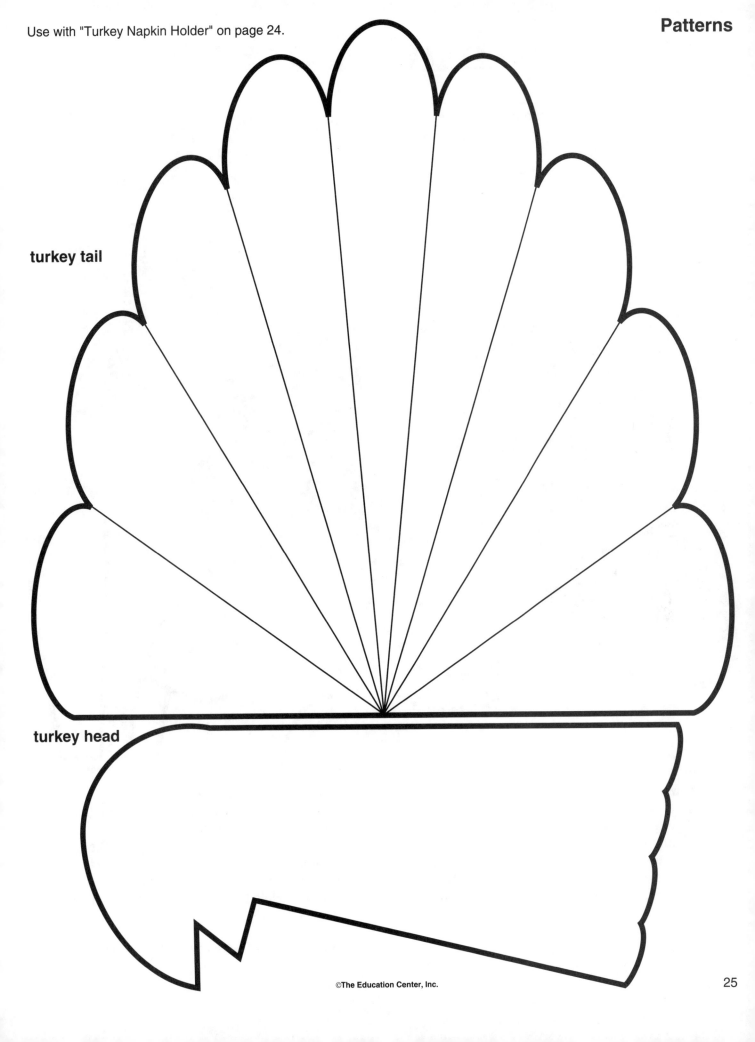

turkey tail

turkey head

# Walnut Turkey

**Materials for one turkey:**

construction paper (red, brown, orange, black)
turkey head, wattle, and feather patterns below
whole walnut
glue
metal bottle cap
scissors
markers

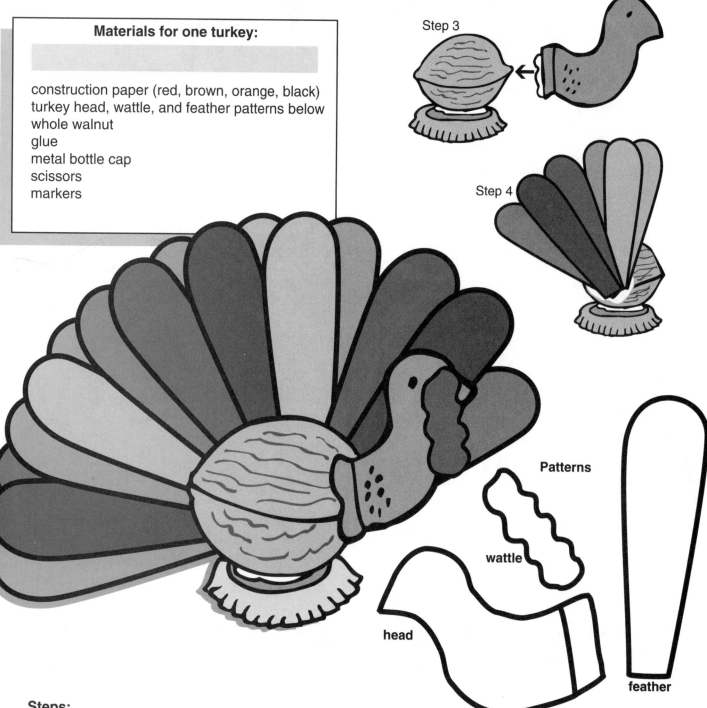

Step 3

Step 4

**Patterns**

wattle

head

feather

## Steps:

1. Glue the walnut to the top of the bottle cap.
2. Use the patterns shown to trace a brown turkey head, a red wattle, and several (15–20) multicolored feathers on construction paper. Cut out the resulting outlines.
3. Decorate the turkey's head using markers.

Fold the bottom of the turkey head cutout as shown. Glue the folded portion to the pointed end of the walnut with glue. (Step 3)
4. Glue the narrow end of each feather to the other end of the walnut in fan fashion (Step 4). Hold the feathers in place until the glue is dry.

*Patsy Greenway—Art Teacher, Foerster Elementary, Houston, TX*

# Leafy Autumn Turkey

## Materials for one turkey:

2 autumn leaves, pressed and dried (one large and one small)
glue
construction paper (yellow, red, and orange)
scissors
black marker
laminating film or clear Con-Tact paper
safety pin (optional)
hot glue gun (optional)

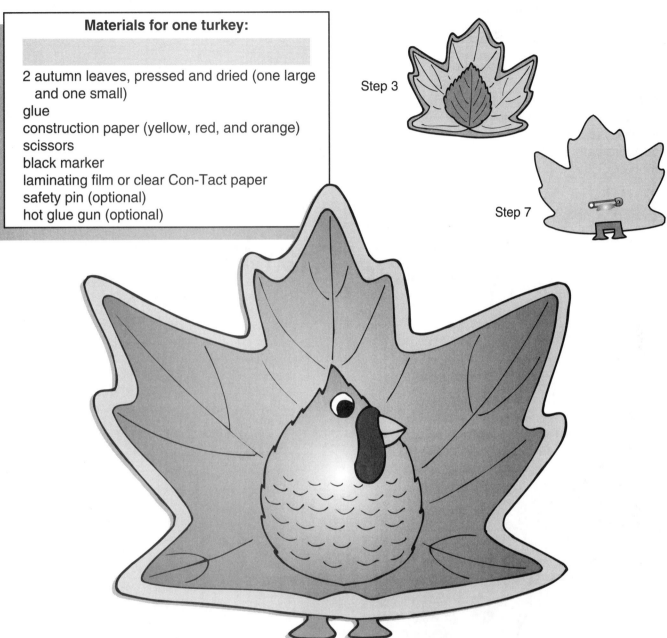

Step 3

Step 7

**Steps:**

1. Glue the large, pressed leaf to a piece of yellow construction paper.
2. Trim the construction paper around the leaf's outer edge, leaving a small border of construction paper.
3. Glue the small leaf to the center of the large leaf as shown (Step 3).
4. From construction paper, cut a red wattle, an orange beak, and orange feet. Then glue the pieces into place on the leaves.
5. Using a black marker, draw an eye and feather marks on the small leaf.
6. Laminate the leaf turkey or cover it with clear Con-Tact paper. Trim the excess laminating film or Con-Tact paper.
7. To make this project into a festive pin, use a hot glue gun to attach a safety pin to the back of the turkey (Step 7). (This step should be done by an adult.)

*Mary Lee Thole—Gr. 1, St. Mary's Public School, Trenton, IL*

# I Am Thankful

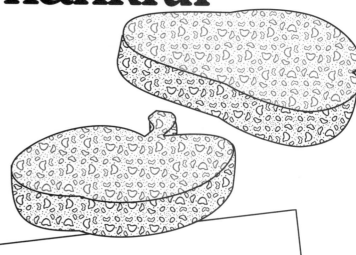

**Materials:**

**cornucopia pattern on page 29**

9" x 12" brown construction paper
scissors
glue
12" x 18" white construction paper
sponges (cut into fruit shapes)
tempera paint (assorted colors)
markers

## We Give Thanks

**Steps:**

1. Using the pattern, trace or duplicate the cornucopia onto brown construction paper. Cut on the resulting outline and glue the shape onto a sheet of white construction paper.

2. Dip the fruit-shaped sponges into appropriate colors of tempera paint and press them gently onto the paper.

3. When the paint is dry, use markers to add details to the cornucopia and the fruit. Label the picture "We Give Thanks."

*Gloria W. Boyd—Gr. K, Riverlawn Elementary, Pulaski County, VA*

cornucopia

# Eye-Catching Indian Corn

**Materials for one project:**

**pattern on page 31**

tagboard
pencil
scissors
tempera paints (red, green, yellow, orange,
   and blue)
3 dried corn husks
glue

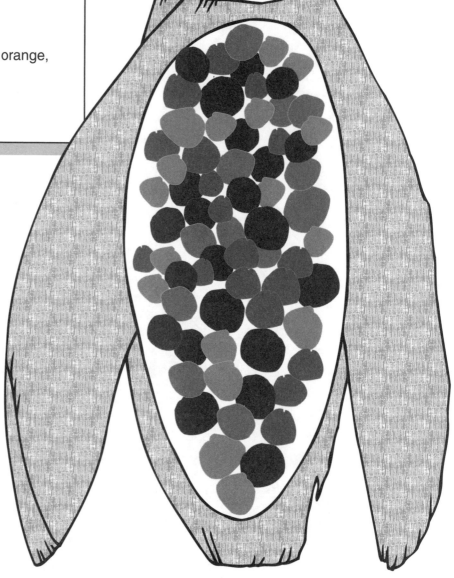

**Steps:**

1. Duplicate or trace the pattern on page 31 on tagboard. Cut out the corn outline.
2. Dip your finger into a color of tempera paint; then press it onto the cutout in several places.
3. Without wiping the paint from your finger, dip your finger into another color of paint and press it onto the cutout several times. Repeat this step until the cutout is covered with multicolored spots. Allow the paint to dry.
4. Glue the dried corn husks to the back of the cutout.

*Jane Ransdell—Grs. K–2, Platte Valley #8 School, North Platte, NE*

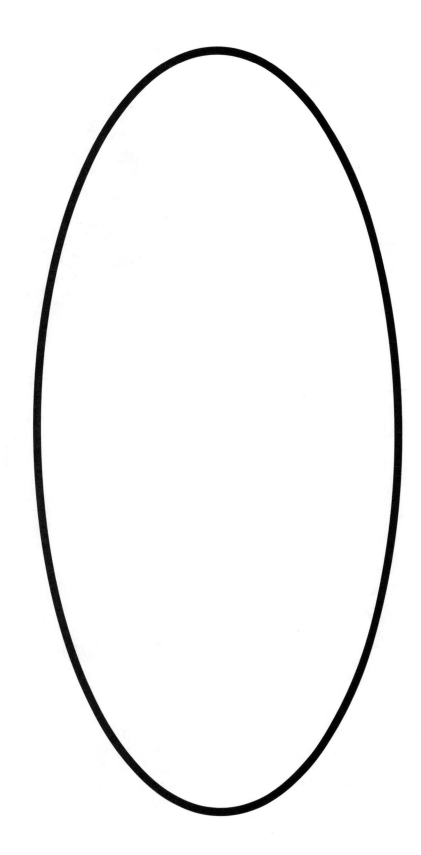

# Christmas Angel

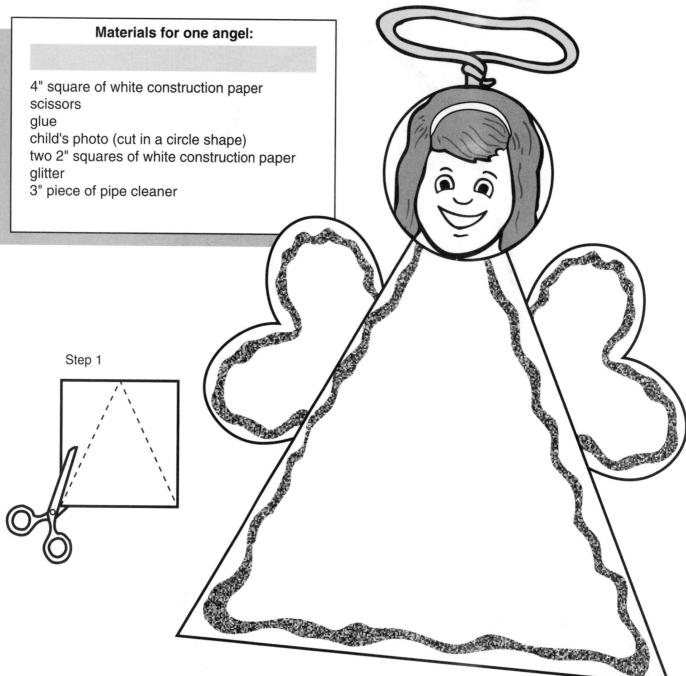

**Materials for one angel:**

4" square of white construction paper
scissors
glue
child's photo (cut in a circle shape)
two 2" squares of white construction paper
glitter
3" piece of pipe cleaner

Step 1

**Steps:**

1. To make the angel's body, cut a triangle from the four-inch square of white construction paper (Step 1).
2. Position the triangle so that one point is at the top. Glue the child's picture to this point of the triangle.
3. Cut a heart from each of two 2-inch squares of white construction paper for arms. Glue the arms in place.
4. Squeeze a trail of glue around the edges of the triangle and hearts. Sprinkle the glue with glitter. Shake off any excess glitter.
5. Shape the piece of pipe cleaner into a halo. Attach the halo to the back of the photo with glue.

*Cassandra A. Carter—Gr. K, Pine Grove Elementary, Shreveport, LA*

# Christmas Note Cards

## Materials for one card:

Christmas cookie cutter
(with details that will
make impressions)
Styrofoam meat tray
square of cardboard
(slightly larger than the
cookie cutter)
ink or tempera paint
sponge

colored paper
(folded like a
card)
scissors
glue

Step 3

**Steps:**

1. Press the cookie cutter into the meat tray. Cut around the cookie cutter's outer edges to trim the excess Styrofoam.
2. Press the Styrofoam shape into the cookie cutter to imprint the shape with details.
3. Glue the shape onto the square of cardboard (Step 3).
4. Dab ink or tempera paint onto the shape with a sponge.
5. Turn the shape facedown on the front of the card and press down firmly on the card board. Carefully lift the shape from the card to reveal a festive design.

*Dolores Daniels—Grs. 5 & 6, North Chili Christian School, North Chili, NY*

# Cone Santa

**Materials for one Santa:**

cone-shaped paper cup
red tempera paint
paintbrush
markers
cotton balls
glue
red or white pom-pom

**Steps:**

1. Position the cup on your work surface so the point is at the top.
2. Using red tempera paint, paint the top half of the cone to make a hat. Let it dry.
3. Below the hat, use markers to draw facial features.
4. Gently pull cotton balls apart just enough to loosen the cotton. Then glue the cotton in place to form a mustache and beard.
5. Glue a pom-pom to the point of the cone to complete the project.

*Laura Stebner—Gr. K, Harry Truman School, Parlin, NJ*

# Not A Creature Was Stirring

## Materials for one project:

½ walnut shell                         glue
cotton
2 small plastic beads
1 fuzzy end of a pussy willow
2 small pinecone scales
fabric scrap
scissors
1" length of ³⁄₁₆-inch-wide ribbon
12" length of ³⁄₁₆-inch-wide ribbon

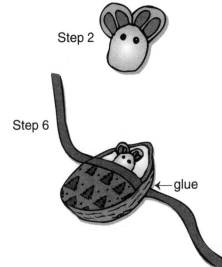

Step 2

Step 6

←glue

## Steps:

1. Tear off a piece of cotton and glue it inside the walnut shell half to make the mouse's bed.
2. To make the mouse, glue two small beads to the pussy willow for eyes. Then glue two small pinecone scales to the back of the pussy willow for ears. (Step 2)
3. Glue the mouse into the bed.
4. Cut a small piece of fabric to fit the walnut shell. Then glue the fabric to the shell as shown to make a blanket.
5. Glue a one-inch piece of ribbon to the top edge of the blanket for trim.
6. Squeeze a one-inch trail of glue in the center of the longer ribbon. Lay the bottom of the walnut shell atop the glue. (Step 6) Press the ribbon to the walnut shell and hold the ribbon in place to dry.
7. Tie the ribbon ends in a bow above the bed to form a loop for suspending the bed.

*Kathy Weimerskirch—Gr. 2, Gage School, Rochester, MN*

# Jingling Doorbells

## Materials:

26" lengths of macramé cord (red or green)
masking tape
3" lengths of yarn
small jingle bells
scissors

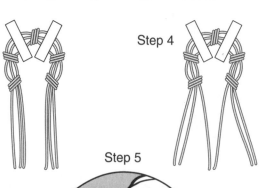

Step 2

Step 3

Step 4

Step 5

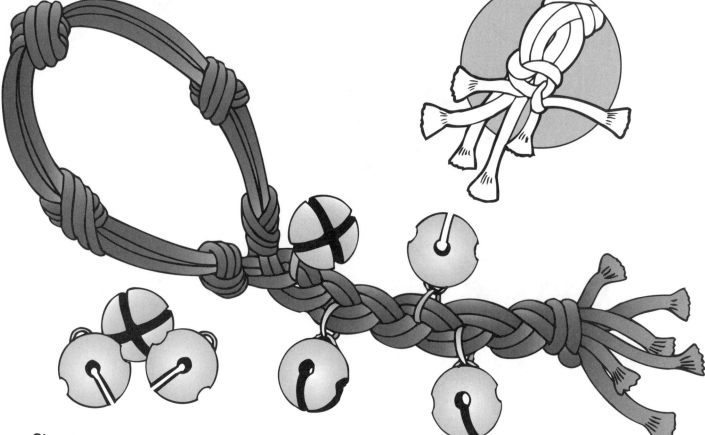

## Steps:

1. Position three macramé cords side by side.
2. Tie the cords together in a knot in the center. On either side of the knot, tie two additional knots 1½ inches apart. (Step 2)
3. Bring the four outer knots together to form an oval as shown. Use masking tape to tape the top of the oval to a tabletop. (Step 3)
4. To prepare for braiding, separate the cords into pairs as shown (Step 4). Braid the cords together.
5. Near the bottom of the braid, wrap two of the cords around the braid and tie them in a knot (Step 5).
6. Thread four or five jingle bells onto lengths of yarn and tie them between the cords of the braid in various places. Trim the excess yarn.

Hang these festive projects on doorknobs for sounds of the holidays!

*Jeanine Peterson—Gr. 2, Bainbridge Elementary, Bainbridge, IN*

# Stand-Out Christmas Tree

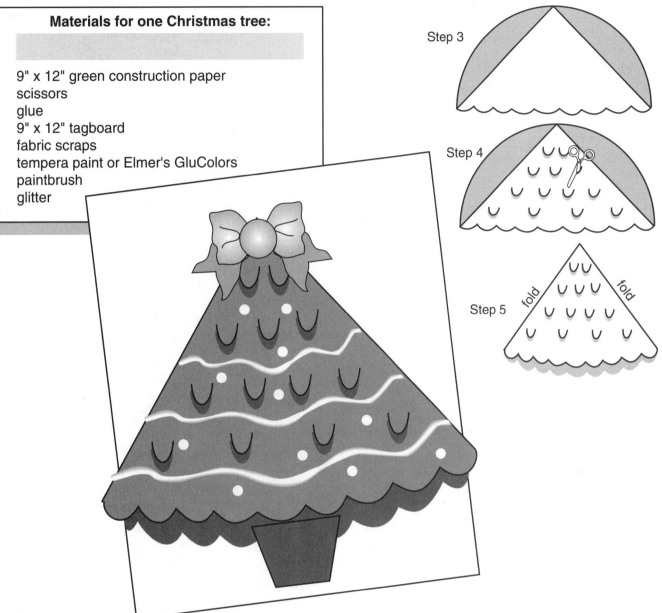

**Materials for one Christmas tree:**

9" x 12" green construction paper
scissors
glue
9" x 12" tagboard
fabric scraps
tempera paint or Elmer's GluColors
paintbrush
glitter

Step 3

Step 4

Step 5

fold          fold

**Steps:**

1. From a sheet of 9" x 12" green construction paper, cut a large semicircle.
2. Cut scallops along the straight edge of the paper.
3. Fold and crease each side of the semicircle as shown in Step 3, forming a triangle in the center of the paper.
4. In various places on the triangle area, cut U-shaped flaps as shown. Bend the flaps up slightly to make them stand out from the tree. (Step 4)

5. Squeeze glue onto the two folded flaps of the tree and attach the flaps to the piece of tagboard, pulling the flaps in slightly to make a three-dimensional half-cone (Step 5). Hold the flaps in place until the glue dries.
6. From fabric scraps, cut a tree trunk, a bow, and other details for the tree. Glue them in place. Add more decorations to the tree with Elmer's GluColors or paint and glitter. Shake off any excess glitter.

*Joan M. Macey, Benjamin Franklin School, Binghamton, NY*

# Angel Ornament

## Materials for one ornament:

one 12" gold chenille stem
¾" unfinished wooden bead
colored Paper Twist (available in most craft
  stores)
white Paper Twist
1" length of thin wire
craft glue
black fine-tip marker
thin string                                scissors

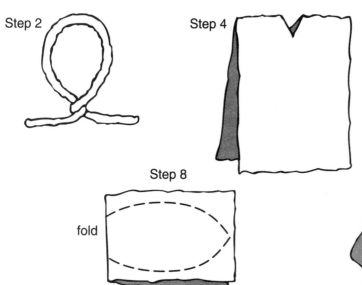

Step 2

Step 4

Step 8

fold

## Steps:

1. Cut the chenille stem into two pieces (3 ¾ inches and 8 ¼ inches).
2. Using the long chenille piece, twist a halo in the center as shown in Step 2. Push the ends of the chenille piece through the wooden bead (the angel's head).
3. Position the halo over the head.
4. Cut a 7 ¼-inch piece of colored Paper Twist and untwist it. Fold the paper in half. Cut a small *V* in the center of the folded edge. (Step 4)
5. Insert the chenille ends into the *V*. Then extend the ends to make the angel's arms.
6. One inch below the arms, gather the Paper Twist together. Twist the remaining chenille piece around the paper to secure the gather, forming the angel's robe. Spread out the bottom of the robe.
7. Cut a two-inch piece of white Paper Twist and untwist it. Fold the paper in half.
8. Cut a wing shape in the folded rectangle as shown in Step 8. Then open the wings and gather the center together with a length of thin wire. Twist the excess wire around the gather.
9. Attach the wings to the back of the angel with glue.
10. Draw facial features on the angel with a fine-tip marker.
11. To suspend the ornament, tie a length of thin string around the angel's neck.

Diane Roberts—Gr. 2, Little Egg Harbor Primary, Little Egg Harbor Township, NJ

# Round Christmas Ornament

**Materials needed for one ornament:**

newspaper
1 paper clip
1 Styrofoam ball
wallpaper paste
absorbent paper towels (cut into 1" strips)
tempera paint (assorted colors)
paintbrush
clear lacquer spray
length of yarn

Step 4

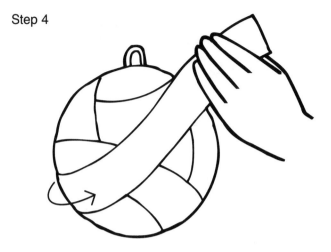

## Steps:

1. Cover your work area with newspaper.
2. Push a paper clip into the top of a Styrofoam ball.
3. Mix the wallpaper paste according to the package directions.
4. Immerse a paper towel strip into the paste and smooth off the excess paste. Then wrap the strip around the Styrofoam ball, smoothing down the edges (Step 4). Repeat this procedure until the ball has been covered completely with two to three layers of paper towel strips. Allow several days for the paste to dry completely.
5. Use tempera paints to paint the ornament with a desired Christmas design.
6. When the paint is dry, spray the ornament with a coat of clear lacquer.
7. To suspend the ornament, tie a length of yarn through the paper clip.

*Kelly Kingsley—Gr. 5, Wake Robin School, Bellevue, NE*

# Christmas Candle

**Materials for one candle:**

paper towel roll
cardboard bowl
red and green tempera paints
paintbrush
glue
1½" yellow construction-paper square
scissors
glitter

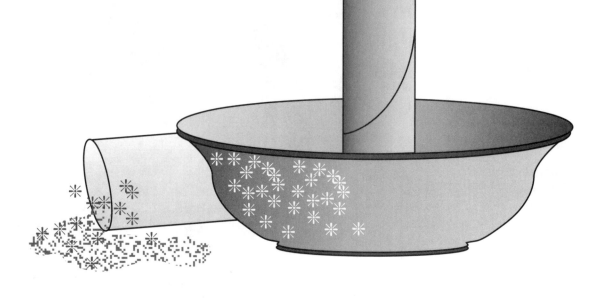

**Steps:**

1. Using the tempera paints, paint the paper towel roll red and the cardboard bowl green. (These colors may be reversed, if desired.) Allow the paint to dry.

2. Spread a coat of glue in the bottom of the bowl; then stand the paper towel roll in the bowl and allow the glue to dry.

3. Cut a triangle from the square of yellow construction paper for the candle flame. Glue the flame to the top of the paper towel roll.

4. To decorate the bowl, glue glitter designs on it. Carefully shake off any excess glitter.

*Donna Ayers—Gr. 1, Brookview Elementary School, Jacksonville, FL*

# Christmas Magnet

**Materials for one magnet:**

2" square of white ceramic tile
fine-tip permanent markers (assorted colors)
2" square of felt
craft glue
magnetic tape
scissors

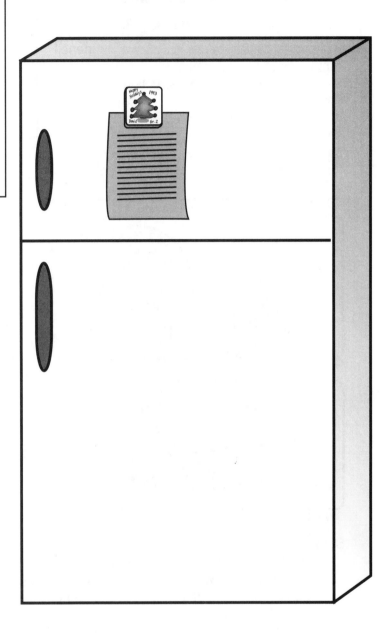

**Steps:**

1. Select and draw a Christmas design on the ceramic tile using permanent markers. Personalize the design as desired. To prevent the colors from bleeding together, allow each color to dry before using a different-color marker.

2. Attach the felt to the back of the tile using craft glue. Let it dry.

3. Attach two 1 1/2-inch strips of magnetic tape to the back of the tile.

*Jeanine Peterson—Gr. 2, Bainbridge Elementary School, Bainbridge, IN*

# Fluffy The Snowman

### Materials for one snowman:

**hat pattern on page 43**

| | |
|---|---|
| white toilet tissue | pencil |
| empty, plastic 2-liter bottle | glue |
| 9" x 12" sheet of black construction paper | |
| scissors | |
| 4" x 12" black construction-paper strip | |
| stapler | |
| construction-paper scraps (assorted colors) | |
| length of crepe-paper streamer (any color) | |

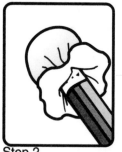

Step 2

Step 5

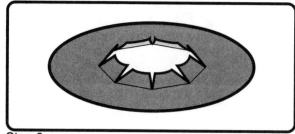

Step 6

## Steps:

1. Tear the toilet tissue into squares.
2. Cover the bottle with toilet tissue by folding each square, one at a time, over the end of a pencil (Step 2).
3. Dab each piece lightly in glue and attach it to the bottle. When the bottle is completely covered, allow the glue to dry.
4. To make the hat, trace the pattern on page 43 onto black construction paper and cut on the resulting outline.
5. Cut out the small circle traced in the center of the hat cutout; then cut 6 to 8 one-inch slits starting from the inside of the small circle to make tabs (Step 5).
6. Bend the tabs up as shown in Step 6.
7. Staple the 4" x 12" strip of construction paper into a cylinder.
8. Place the cylinder atop the black circle and glue the tabs inside the cylinder. Glue the hat to the top of the bottle.
9. Cut out facial features and buttons from construction paper; then glue these pieces in place on the snowman.
10. Gently tie a length of crepe-paper streamer around the snowman for a scarf. Snip the ends of the streamer with scissors to make fringe.

To use this snowman as a doorstop, fill the bottle with sand.

*Janis Woods—Gr. K, Ridgeland Elementary School, Ridgeland, SC*

Use with "Fluffy The Snowman" on page 42.

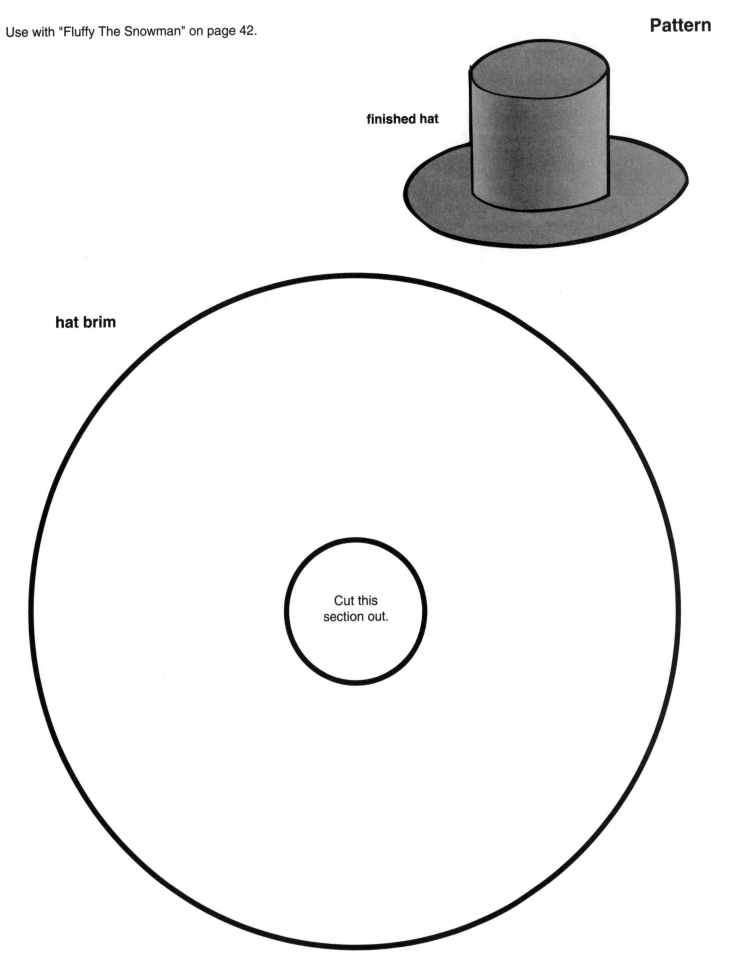

finished hat

hat brim

Cut this
section out.

# Wooden Snowman

**Materials for one snowman:**

**patterns on page 45**

precut wooden snowman shape
  (using the patterns on page 45)
craft paint (cream, black, and orange)
paintbrush
1 toothpick
scissors
1" x 18" strip of felt
glue
2 thin twigs (each approximately 2 ½" long)

## Steps:

*(Prior to this project, have a parent who is familiar with woodworking use the patterns on page 45 to cut out wooden snowmen from 2" x 4" wood scraps. Then, in each wooden snowman, have the parent drill a very small hole [to hold a toothpick in place] for the snowman's nose. [See the dot on each pattern.] Next have him drill 1/4-inch holes on either side of the snowman for the twig arms.)*

1. Use cream-colored craft paint to paint the entire snowman. Let it dry for approximately 20 minutes.
2. Paint the top of the snowman black as shown to make his hat.
3. Paint two black dots for eyes.
4. While the paint is drying, break the toothpick in half and paint it orange for a carrot nose. Let the toothpick dry.
5. Use scissors to notch the ends of the felt for fringe. Tie the strip of felt around the snowman's neck for a scarf. Squeeze a few drops of glue under the felt to secure it in place.
6. Put a few drops of glue on the ends of the twigs and position the twigs in the armholes.
7. Put the toothpick nose into its hole with a drop of glue.

*Peggy Murray—Gr. K, Houlton Elementary, Houlton, WI*

Use with "Wooden Snowman" on page 44.

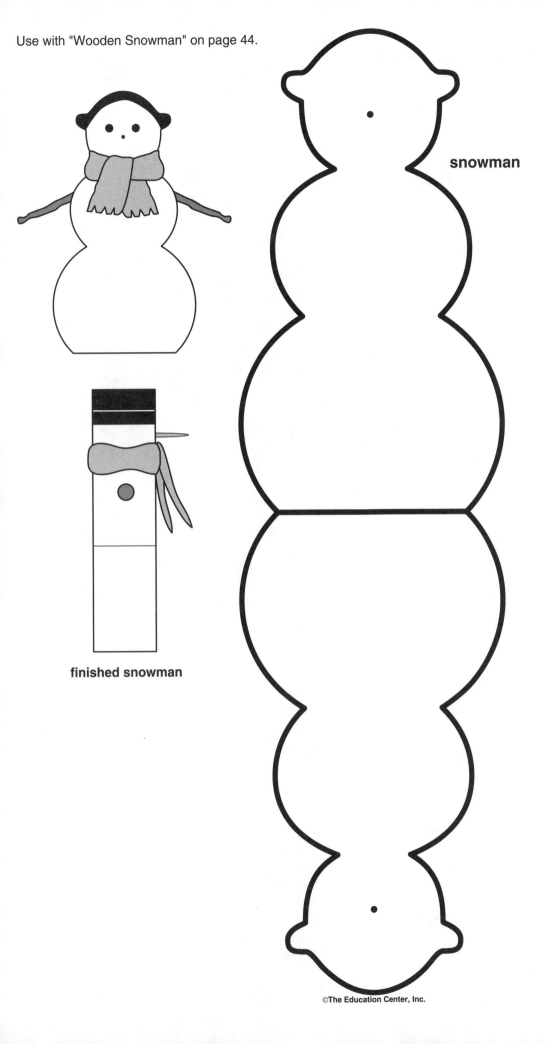

**snowman**

**finished snowman**

# Wintry Pine Tree Scene

**Materials for one project:**

2 sponges　　　　　　　　　　scissors
tempera paints (green and white)
9" x 12" blue construction paper
4" pine-tree clippings
white construction paper
glue
construction-paper scraps (assorted colors)
markers (black, orange, and brown)
silver glitter

Step 3

Step 6

**Steps:**

1. Saturate each sponge with a color of tempera paint (one green and one white).
2. Position a sheet of blue construction paper vertically.
3. Press a pine-tree clipping into the sponge saturated with green paint. Then press the clipping onto the blue construction paper to make part of the tree. (Step 3)
4. Repeat Step 3 several times, pressing the clipping in various places to form a pine tree. Allow the paint to dry.
5. Press another pine-tree clipping into the sponge saturated with white paint. Press this clipping gently atop the pine tree in various places to make a light covering of snow. Allow the paint to dry.

6. Using white construction paper, tear several strips and glue them to the base of the paper to make snow. Trim the edges if necessary. (Step 6)
7. Tear out a snowman shape from white construction paper and glue it next to the pine tree. From assorted colors of construction-paper scraps, tear out a hat and a scarf. Glue these pieces onto the snowman.
8. Using markers, add black coal eyes and mouth, a carrot nose, black coal buttons, and brown stick arms. Color a brown trunk at the base of the pine tree.
9. Complete the scene by putting several dots of glue atop the picture. Sprinkle the glue with silver glitter. Shake off the excess glitter to reveal sparkling snowflakes.

*Mary Lee Thole—Gr. 1,*
*St. Mary's Public School, Trenton, IL*

# Tie-Dyed Valentine Card

### Materials for one card:

9" x 12" construction paper (red or pink)
pencil
pattern for tracing (optional)
scissors
food coloring (assorted colors)
water
small containers
1 absorbent paper towel
glue

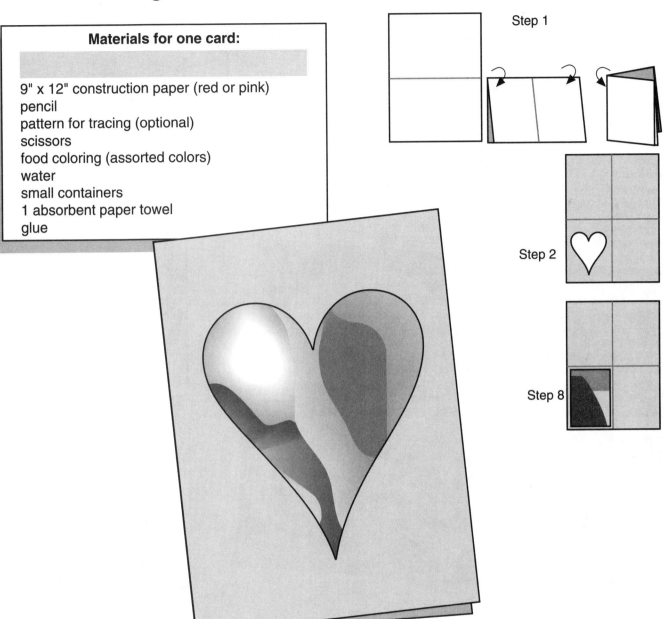

Step 1

Step 2

Step 8

**Steps:**

1. Fold the construction paper into a card as shown in Step 1. Then unfold the card.
2. On the back side of the front section of the card, draw or trace a desired pattern. Cut on the outline and set the card aside. (Step 2)
3. Fill several small containers with food coloring and water, one color per container.
4. Fold the paper towel in half. Continue to fold the paper towel in half until it is approximately a 1 1/2-inch square.
5. Dip each corner of the paper-towel square into a different color of food coloring. Allow the colors to bleed together on the paper towel.
6. Carefully unfold the paper towel and allow it to dry.
7. Cut out a section of the dyed paper towel slightly larger than the cut-out area on the card.
8. Glue the paper-towel cutout behind the front of the card to cover the cut-out area (Step 8). Fold the paper into a card again.

*Dolores Daniels—Grs. 5 & 6, North Chili Christian School, North Chili, NY*

# Window Valentines

## Materials for one project:

### heart pattern on page 49

two 9" x 12" sheets of black construction paper
pencil
scissors
one 9" x 12" sheet of white tissue paper
glue
diluted glue
paintbrush
plastic grocery bag
tissue-paper scraps (red, white, and pink)

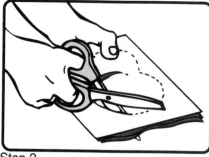

Step 2

Step 6

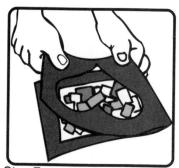

Step 7

## Steps:

1. Stack the sheets of black construction paper and align the edges.
2. Position the pattern on page 49 in the center of the top sheet of paper and trace it. Push the point of the scissors through the papers at the edge of the heart and cut out the outline through both sheets of construction paper. (Be sure not to cut from the edge of the paper. This will be the border of the project.) (Step 2)
3. Discard the cut-out pieces.
4. Set one of the heart windows aside. Spread a coat of glue on the other heart window around the cut-out area. Place the sheet of white tissue paper atop the glue, aligning the edges.
5. Spread out the plastic grocery bag. Place the heart window atop the plastic with the tissue-paper sheet faceup. Brush a coat of diluted glue over the tissue paper.
6. Cut red, pink, and white pieces of tissue paper into desired shapes. Arrange the tissue-paper pieces atop the glue, overlapping the edges. (Brush on more diluted glue if needed.) Allow the glue to dry. (Step 6)
7. Glue the remaining heart window atop the project, aligning the windows (Step 7).

Attach your students' projects in a sunny window for a beautiful display.

*Dolores Daniels—Grs. 5 & 6,*
*North Chili Christian School, North Chili, NY*

Use with "Window Valentines" on page 48, "Hearts Of Color" on page 51, and "Patriotic Hearts" on page 53.

# Valentine Spatter Painting

**Materials for one picture:**

food coloring
water
plastic containers
heart cutouts (various sizes)
white construction paper
strainer (or colander)
toothbrush

Step 2

Step 4

**Steps:**
*(While making this project, be sure to wear a smock to protect your clothing.)*

1. In each of several plastic containers, mix water and a different color of food coloring.
2. Arrange the heart cutouts atop a sheet of white construction paper as desired (Step 2).
3. Invert the strainer (or colander) atop the construction paper.
4. Dip the toothbrush into a desired food coloring mixture; then brush the toothbrush over the top of the strainer, spattering color on the picture. Continue in this manner, using a variety of colors. (Step 4)
5. When the desired look is achieved, remove the strainer and the heart cutouts. Allow the picture to dry.

*Jean Potter, Charleston, WV*

# Hearts Of Color

**Materials for one project:**

**pattern on page 49**

tagboard
scissors
9" x 12" white paper
oil pastels
bathroom tissue

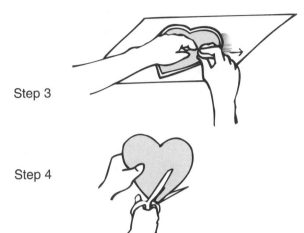

Step 3

Step 4

**Steps:**

1. Duplicate the pattern on page 49 on tagboard. Cut out the resulting outline for a tracer.
2. Position the tracer atop the white paper. Using a desired color of oil pastel, trace a thick line along the tracer's outer edge.
3. Continue to hold the tracer in place. Then, using a square of bathroom tissue, smear the line of oil pastel in outward strokes. (Step 3)
4. Using scissors, trim the tracer to a slightly smaller size. Place the tracer in the center of the heart. Using a different color of oil pastel, repeat steps 2 and 3. (Step 4)
5. Repeat Step 4 several times until the project is complete.

*Beth Jones—Grs. 1 & 2, General Vanier School, Niagara Falls, Ontario, Canada*

# Valentine Gift Bow

## Materials for one project:

5" square of fabric (valentine color or design)
sewing machine or pinking shears
rigatoni pasta
tempera paint
paintbrush
safety pin
hot glue gun

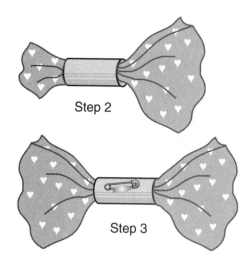

Step 2

Step 3

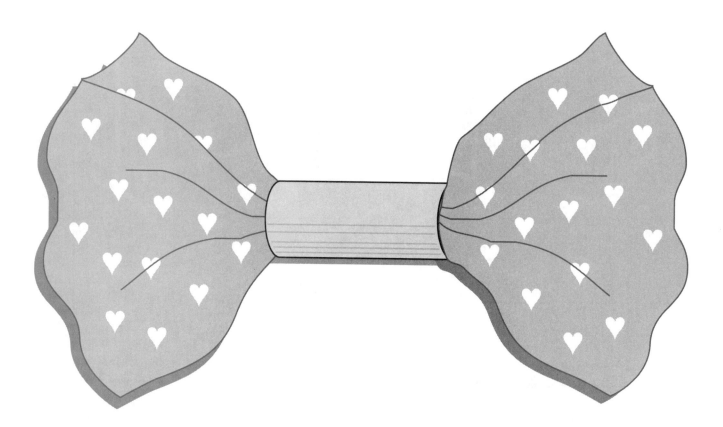

**Steps:**
*(Prior to doing this project, hem the edges of each fabric square or cut them with pinking shears to prevent fraying.)*

1. Paint one piece of rigatoni pasta with tempera paint and allow the paint to dry.

2. Pull the fabric square through the pasta as shown in Step 2. Arrange the fabric on either side of the pasta, forming a bow.

3. Using a hot glue gun, glue the safety pin to the back of the pasta (Step 3). (This step should be done by an adult.)

*Jean Potter, Charleston, WV*

# Patriotic Hearts

## Materials for one project:

### pattern on page 49

pencil
9" x 12" construction paper (red, white, and blue)
scissors
glue
1" white tissue-paper squares
star hole puncher (White star stickers or a white crayon can also be used to make stars.)

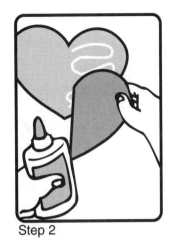
Step 2

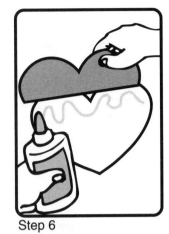
Step 6

**Steps:**

1. Using the pattern on page 49, trace a heart onto red construction paper. Cut out the resulting outline.
2. Fold the pattern in half and trace half of a heart onto blue construction paper. Cut out the resulting outline and glue it atop one-half of the red heart, aligning the edges. (Step 2)
3. To make stripes on the heart, crumple white tissue-paper squares—one at a time—into loose balls. Then glue them in rows across the red half of the heart.
4. Using a star hole puncher, punch several star shapes from white construction paper. Glue the stars to the blue half of the heart. (If a star hole puncher is not available, use white star stickers or draw stars with a white crayon.)

**Variation:**

5. To make a different style of heart, trace the heart pattern onto white construction paper and then cut it out.
6. Trace the upper half of the heart pattern onto blue construction paper. Cut out the resulting outline and glue it atop the white heart, aligning the edges. (Step 6)
7. Glue rows of red tissue-paper-ball stripes to the lower half of the heart by using the technique described in Step 3.
8. Attach white stars to the upper half of the heart to complete the project.

*Mary Lee Thole—Gr. 1,*
*St. Mary's Public School, Trenton, IL*

# Valentine Flower

**Materials:**

**heart patterns on page 55**

construction paper (red, white, pink, and green)
scissors
9" paper plates
glue
heart pattern below
pencils

**Pattern**

Step 4

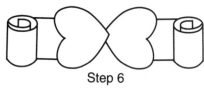

Step 6

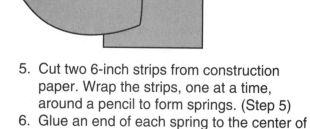

**Steps:**

1. Duplicate the heart patterns on page 55 onto red, white, and pink construction paper.
2. Select and cut out six hearts in any desired colors. Glue these hearts to the outer edge of a paper plate.
3. Using the pattern shown, trace four hearts onto red, pink, or white construction paper. Cut on the resulting outlines.
4. Roll the top section of each heart loosely around a pencil as shown (Step 4). Then glue the point of each heart to the center of the paper plate.
5. Cut two 6-inch strips from construction paper. Wrap the strips, one at a time, around a pencil to form springs. (Step 5)
6. Glue an end of each spring to the center of the paper plate. Then cut out two small construction-paper hearts and glue them atop the springs. (Step 6)
7. Cut out and glue other valentine designs as desired.
8. From green construction paper, cut out a stem and leaves. Glue the leaves to the stem; then glue the top of the stem to the back of the paper plate.

*Lynda Neuroth, Johnson School, Livonia, MI*

**Patterns**

# Lucky Leprechaun

**Materials for one leprechaun:**

**patterns on pages 57 and 58**

12" x 18" construction paper
  (1 green and 1 white)
pencil
scissors
4" x 6" piece of black
  construction paper
glue
crayon (red or pink)

green yarn
stapler
tape

Step 1

Step 3

Step 4

Step 5

Step 10

## Steps:

1. Fold the sheet of green construction paper in half. Trace the hat pattern on page 57 on the green construction paper, lining up the long edge of the pattern with the fold. (Step 1) Cut on the resulting outline and unfold the hat shape.
2. Cut a three-inch square from black construction paper for a buckle.
3. Fold the black square in half and cut a smaller square on the fold as shown in Step 3. Open the buckle and glue it to the center of the hat.
4. Fold the sheet of white construction paper in half. Line up the beard pattern (on page 58) with the fold as shown in Step 4 and trace the pattern. Cut out and unfold the resulting outline.
5. Squeeze a dot of glue onto each end of the beard and attach the beard to the hat (Step 5).
6. Using a crayon, draw a mouth in the center of the beard.
7. Cut two 2 1/2-inch circles from white construction paper for the eyes.
8. To the center of each white circle, glue a one-inch, black construction-paper circle.
9. Cut two 3-inch lengths of yarn. Staple an eye to the end of each length of yarn.
10. Attach the eyes to the leprechaun by taping the opposite end of each length of yarn to the back of the hat (Step 10).

*Meghan G. Devito—Gr. K, Pequenakonck School, North Salem, NY*

**hat pattern**

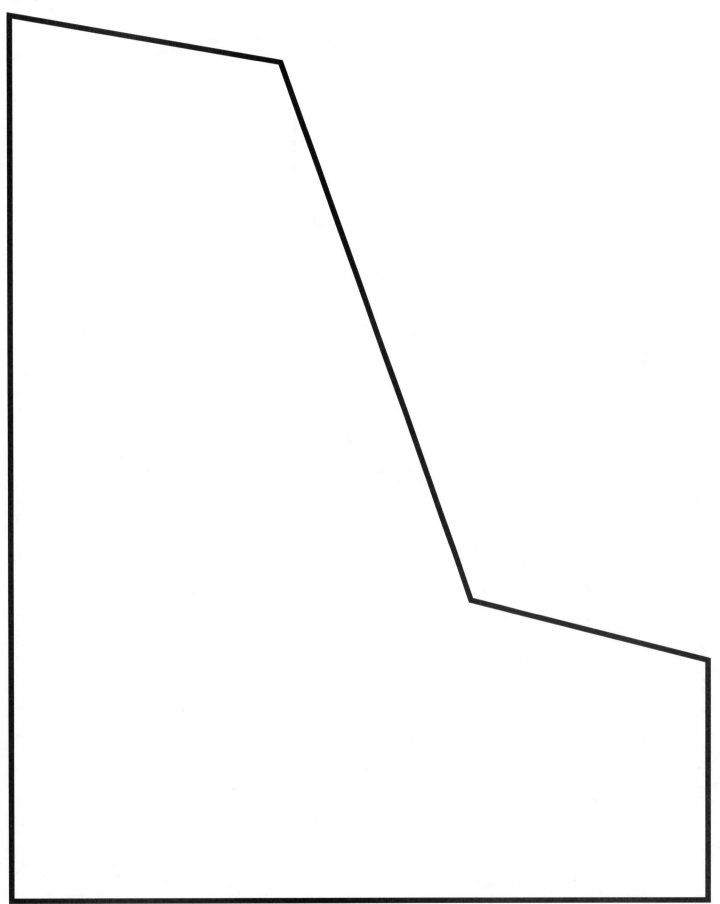

# Pattern

Use with "Lucky Leprechaun" on page 56.

**beard pattern**

# March Lion

**Materials for one lion:**

paper plate
Styrofoam packing pieces
glue
yellow spray paint or tempera paint
paintbrush
construction paper (yellow, black, and white)
scissors
black marker

Step 5

**Steps:**

1. Glue Styrofoam packing pieces to the outer edge of the paper plate.
2. Allow the glue to dry completely.
3. Paint the plate and the packing pieces. (If you're using tempera paint, use thick paint on the Styrofoam pieces.) Let the paint dry.
4. Cut ears from yellow construction paper and glue them to the back of the plate.
5. Glue on eyes made from white and black construction paper (Step 5).
6. Using black construction paper, cut out and glue on a nose.
7. Draw a mouth and whiskers using the black marker.

*Susan Voss—Gr. 1, Knapp Elementary School, Michigan City, IN*

# March Lion Kite

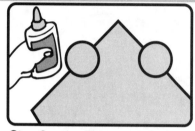

Step 2

Step 3

*(Prior to this art project, copy the patterns on page 61 onto construction paper. Cut out the patterns for students to use as tracers.)*

**Steps:**

1. Trace one diamond and two circles from the patterns on page 61 onto yellow tagboard. Cut on the resulting outlines.
2. Glue the circles to the back of the diamond shape as shown in Step 2.
3. Cut the tissue paper into 4" x 2" rectangles. Glue the ends of the rectangles to the back of the diamond, alternating colors. (Step 3)
4. Attach the two-foot yellow streamer to the bottom point of the diamond.
5. Using the pattern on page 61, trace three bows onto different colors of construction-paper squares. Cut on the resulting outlines.
6. Write the message "March Is Here" on the bows as shown and attach them in order on the streamer.
7. From the black construction-paper squares, cut two triangles for eyes and one oval for a nose. Glue the facial features to the diamond. Use markers to add a mouth and whiskers.
8. Using a hole puncher, punch a hole in the top point of the diamond. Thread and knot a length of yarn through the hole for suspending the kite.

*Kathleen Miller—Gr. K, Our Lady Of Mount Carmel, Tenafly, NJ*

Use with "March Lion Kite" on page 60.

**diamond**

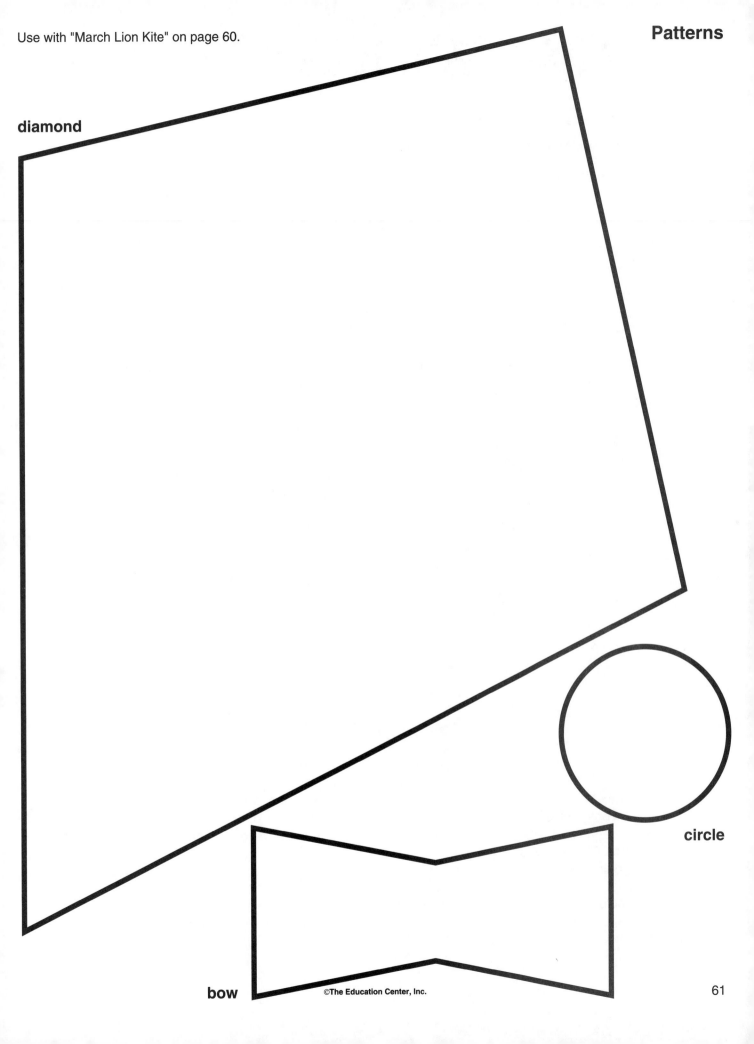

**circle**

**bow**

# Egg With A Chick

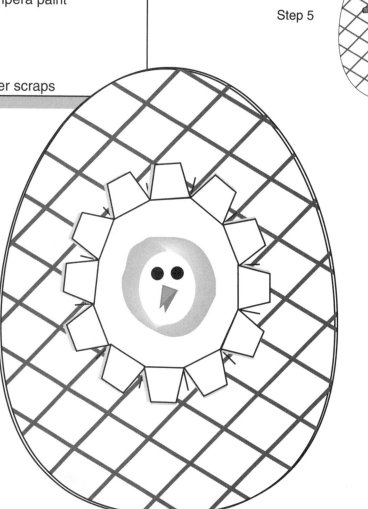

**Materials for one egg:**

**egg pattern on page 65**

12" x 18" white construction paper
scissors
crayons
watercolors or diluted tempera paint
paintbrush
pencil
glue
yellow cotton ball
colored construction-paper scraps

Step 4

Step 5

**Steps:**

1. Fold the 12" x 18" piece of white construction paper in half. Use the pattern on page
   65 to trace an egg shape. Cut the paper to
   make two egg cutouts of equal size.
2. Set one egg cutout aside. On the other egg,
   color heavily to make designs.
3. Brush paint over the egg to make a crayon
   resist; let it dry.
4. Make cuts in the middle of the egg as shown
   (Step 4).
5. Roll back each resulting triangle piece with a
   pencil (Step 5).

6. Take the plain egg cutout and put a trail of
   glue along the edge.
7. Place the decorated egg atop the glue; align
   the edges of both cutouts.
8. Glue the yellow cotton ball in the center of
   the egg.
9. Attach eyes and a folded beak made from
   colored construction-paper scraps.

*Sherry A. Fenton—Gr. 2, Ernest Stapleton Elementary,
Rio Rancho, NM*

# Spring "Chirpees"

Pattern

| Materials for one project: |
| --- |
| **nest pattern shown** |
| 6" x 4" rectangle of brown construction paper |
| pencil |
| scissors |
| 7" rectangle of light blue tagboard |
| glue |
| 2 white or yellow cotton balls |
| 4 wiggly eyes |
| orange construction-paper scrap |
| chow mein noodles |

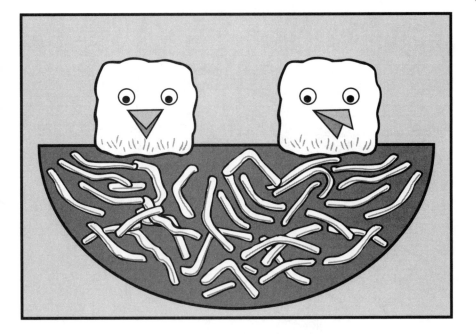

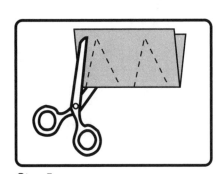

Step 5

## Steps:

1. To make a nest, trace the nest pattern shown on brown construction paper. Cut out the resulting outline.
2. Glue the nest onto the tagboard near the bottom edge.
3. Glue both cotton balls along the straight edge of the nest.
4. Glue a pair of wiggle eyes to each cotton ball.

5. Fold a small piece of orange construction paper in half. Cut two small triangles on the fold to make beaks. (Step 5) Glue the beaks to the cotton balls to complete the chicks.
6. Spread a coat of glue on the nest and sprinkle it with chow mein noodles. Let the glue dry.

*Sally A. Wolfe—Gr. 1, Washington Elementary School, Allentown, PA*

# Exotic Eggs

## Materials for one egg:

### egg pattern on page 65

9" x 12" piece of wallpaper
pencil
scissors
9" x 12" pastel construction paper
glue

Step 2

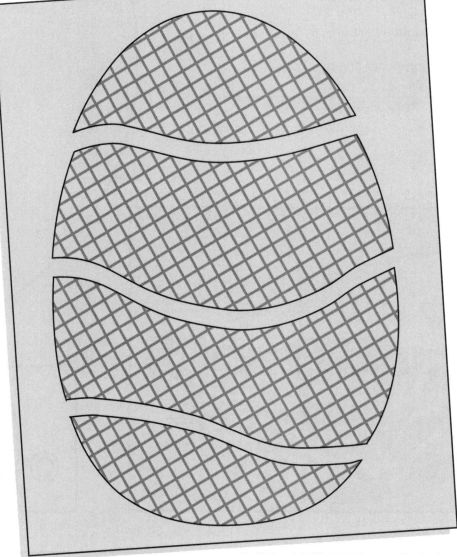

**Steps:**

1. Trace the egg pattern on page 65 onto the back side of the piece of wallpaper. Cut on the resulting outline.
2. On the back of the egg cutout, draw two to five wavy, straight, or zigzag lines. Cut the egg apart on these lines. (Step 2)

3 Turn the resulting pieces faceup. Assemble the egg pieces on the sheet of pastel construction paper. Glue the pieces in place, leaving ¼-inch to ½-inch spaces between the pieces.

*Audrey Biccum—Gr. 4, Panola Way Elementary, Stone Mountain, GA*

Use with "Egg With A Chick" on page 62, "Exotic Eggs" on page 64, and "Giant Stuffed Easter Eggs" on page 69.

**Pattern**

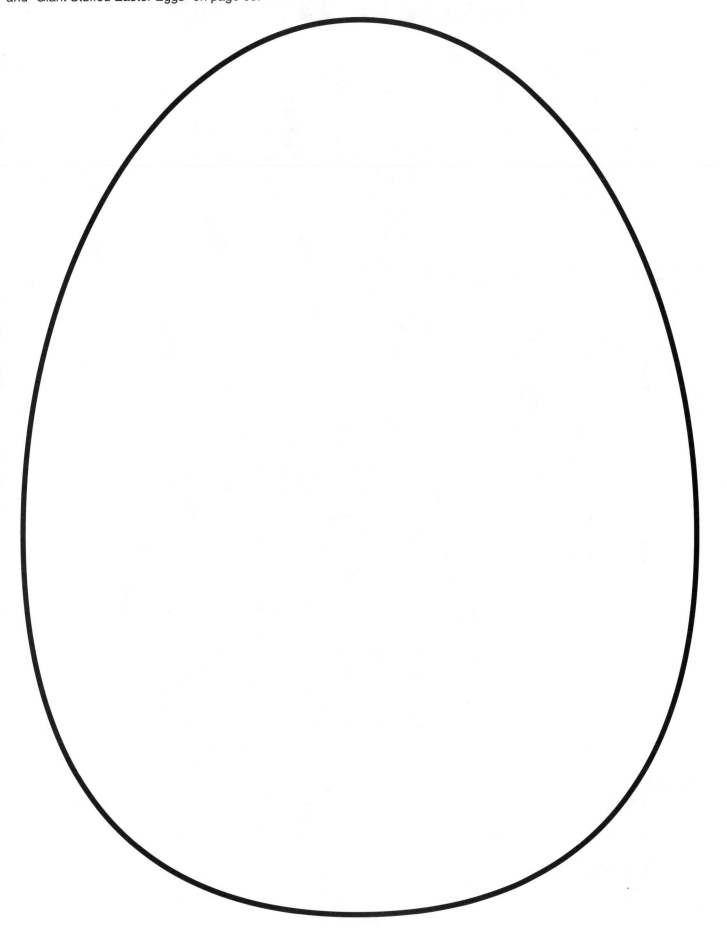

# Stuffed Bunny

**Materials for one bunny:**

paper lunch bag
scissors
newspaper
two 12" lengths of yarn
construction-paper scraps
glue
cotton ball

Step 1

**Steps:**

1. Keeping the bag flat, cut a triangle from the top of the lunch bag to make ears (Step 1).
2. Open the bag and fill it with crumpled newspaper.
3. Gather each ear at the base and tie it with a length of yarn.
4. Glue bunny facial features cut from construction paper to the front of the bag.
5. Glue a cotton ball to the back of the bag for a tail.

*Barbara Williams—Gr. 3, Bel Air Elementary, Evans, GA*

# Bunny Basket

**Materials for one basket:**

**pattern on page 68**

2 sheets of 9" x 12" white construction paper
pencil
scissors
stapler
construction-paper scraps
glue
1 pair of wiggle eyes
crayons or markers
cellophane grass (optional)

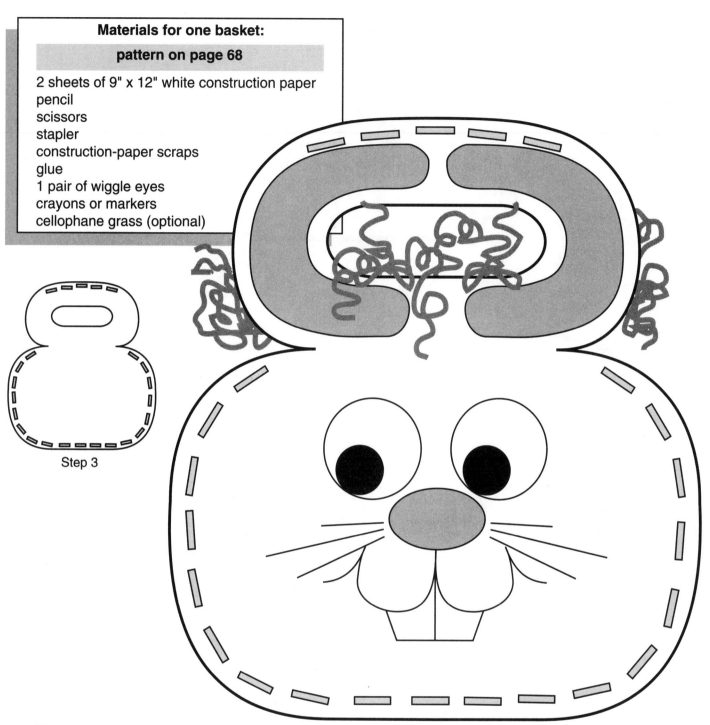

Step 3

**Steps:**

1. Trace or duplicate the pattern on page 68 on both sheets of white construction paper. Cut out the resulting outlines.
2. Stack the cutouts atop one another, aligning the edges.
3. Staple the cutouts together as shown in Step 3. (This should be done with the help of an adult.)
4. From construction-paper scraps, cut out bunny facial features. Glue the pieces in place on the lower section of the basket. Then glue on the wiggle eyes.
5. Use crayons or markers to add color and finishing details to the basket.
6. If desired, fill the basket with cellophane grass.

Use with "Bunny Basket" on page 67.

# Giant Stuffed Easter Eggs

<table>
<tr><td colspan="2">Materials for one egg:</td></tr>
<tr><td colspan="2">pattern on page 65</td></tr>
<tr><td>opaque projector</td><td></td></tr>
<tr><td colspan="2">two 3' lengths of white bulletin-board paper</td></tr>
<tr><td>pencil</td><td></td></tr>
<tr><td>paper clips</td><td></td></tr>
<tr><td>scissors</td><td></td></tr>
<tr><td>crayons</td><td></td></tr>
<tr><td>watercolor paints</td><td>stapler</td></tr>
<tr><td>paintbrush</td><td>newspaper</td></tr>
<tr><td>length of clear fishing line</td><td>hole puncher</td></tr>
</table>

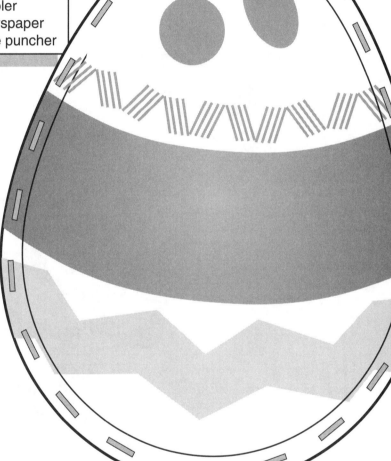

Step 3

## Steps:

1. Using the opaque projector and the pattern on page 65, draw a large egg shape on a three-foot length of white bulletin-board paper. Clip this paper atop the other length of bulletin-board paper. Cut out the resulting outline.

2. Using crayons and watercolors, decorate one side of each egg cutout. Allow the paint to dry.

3. Stack the eggs, plain sides together; then staple them together along the edges, leaving a six-inch opening (Step 4). (This should be done with the help of an adult.)

4. Stuff the egg with crumpled newspaper; then staple the opening closed.

5. Using a hole puncher, punch a hole in the top of the egg. Attach a length of clear fishing line for suspending the egg.

*T. W. McKenzie, Aliquippa, PA*

# Spring Seed Mosaic

### Materials for one project:

9" x 12" piece of cardboard
9" x 12" sheet of construction paper (any color)
glue
pencil
an assortment of seeds (such as birdseed,
    sunflower seeds, or grass seed)

Step 2

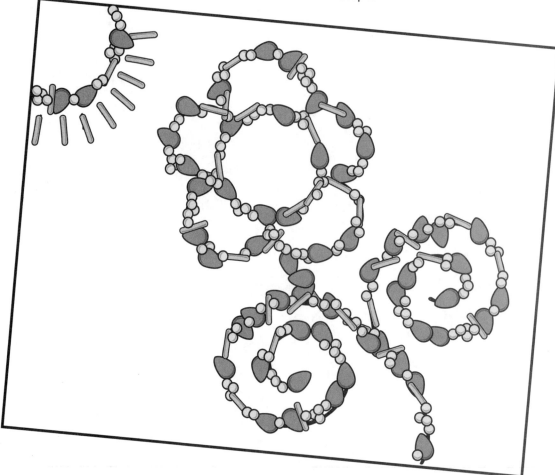

## Steps:

1. Glue a sheet of construction paper in a desired color to one side of the cardboard, aligning the edges.

2. Using a pencil, draw an outline of a simple spring picture (such as a flower, bird, or butterfly) as shown in Step 2.

3. Spread a coat of glue over a small section of the picture. Sprinkle a desired type of seed atop the glue. Continue in this manner until the entire outline is filled with seeds. Allow the glue to dry. Shake off the excess seeds.

*T. W. McKenzie, Aliquippa, PA*

# Sunny Sunflower

**Materials for one project:**

**pattern on page 72**

9" x 12" green construction paper
scissors
9" paper plate
yellow tempera paint
paintbrush
dark-colored marker
glue
hole puncher
length of string

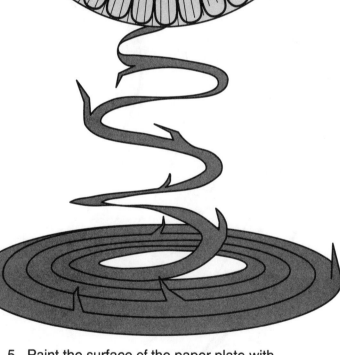

Step 2

Step 3

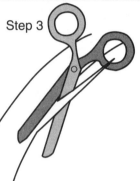

Step 4

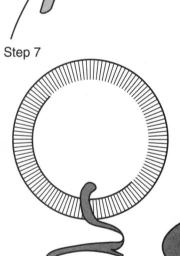 

Step 7

## Steps:

1. Duplicate the pattern on page 72 on green construction paper. Cut along the circle's outer edge.
2. To make the stem, begin cutting a spiral on the dotted line at the point where the dotted line meets the outer edge of the circle. Continue cutting until the dotted line ends. (Step 2)
3. To make leaves, cut on the short dark lines along the stem (Step 3).
4. Bend the leaves as shown in Step 4. Set the completed stem aside.
5. Paint the surface of the paper plate with yellow tempera paint. Allow the paint to dry.
6. Using a marker, draw sunflower petals around the edge of the paper plate. Then draw a face in the center of the plate.
7. Glue one end of the stem to the back of the paper plate (Step 7).
8. Using a hole puncher, punch a hole in the top of the paper plate. Attach a length of string to the hole for suspending the sunflower.

*T. W. McKenzie, Aliquippa, PA*

Use with "Sunny Sunflower" on page 71.

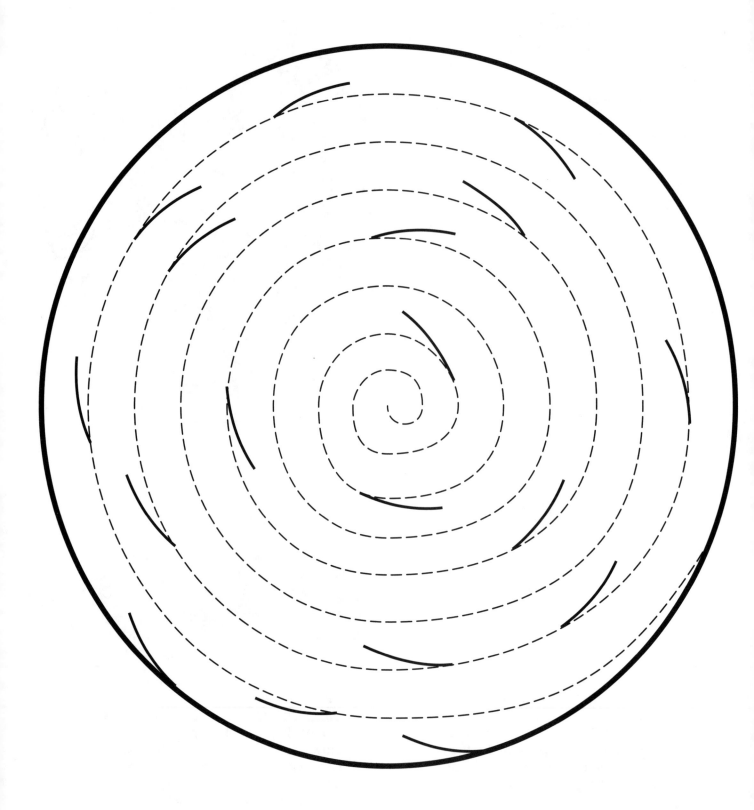

# A Frilly Picture Frame

**Materials for one frame:**

Styrofoam meat tray (washed)
child's photograph (preferably 3" x 5" to 5" x 7")
pencil
scissors
glue                buttons
ribbon              alphabet cereal
yarn                paper clip
lace
fabric scraps

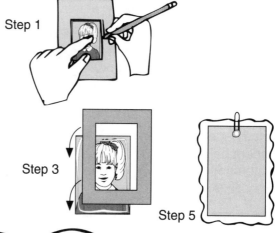

Step 1

Step 3

Step 5

I LOVE YOU!

**Steps:**

1. On the back of the meat tray, center the child's photograph and trace around its outline (Step 1).
2. Cut approximately ¼ inch inside the traced line.
3. Squeeze a trail of glue around the edge on the front of the photograph. Position the back of the meat tray on the glue, centering the photograph in the cut-out area. (Step 3)
4. Decorate the front of the frame with fabric scraps, buttons, ribbon, yarn, and lace. Attach alphabet cereal letters to personalize the frame.
5. Glue the paper clip to the back of the frame as shown to hang it  (Step 5).

These picture-perfect frames make wonderful gifts!

*Linda Sowa—Gr. Gifted Pre-K, Millikin School, Cleveland Heights, OH*

# Cinnamon Gifts

**Materials:**

12 ounces of ground cinnamon
2 cups of applesauce
mixing bowl
cookie cutters
waxed paper
tempera paints
paintbrush
magnetic tape

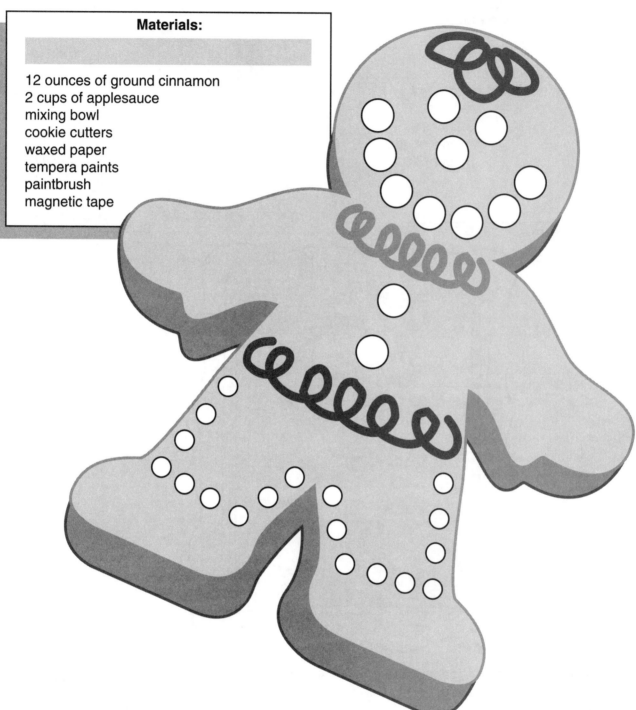

**Steps:**

1. Mix the ground cinnamon and applesauce in the mixing bowl to make dough that is dark brown and slightly wet.
2. Pat the dough onto waxed paper until it is flat. Cut a shape from the dough with a cookie cutter. Place the cut-out shape on another piece of waxed paper to dry. (Drying takes approximately three to five days.)
3. Paint the shape when it has dried completely. Let the paint dry.
4. Apply magnetic tape to the back of the project to display it on metal surfaces.

*Diane Stricek—Gr. K, MacArthur School, Binghamton, NY*

74

# Crayon Box Frame

**Materials for one picture frame:**

child's photograph
clear Con-Tact paper
scissors
tagboard
glue
empty, large crayon box
glitter
12" length of yarn

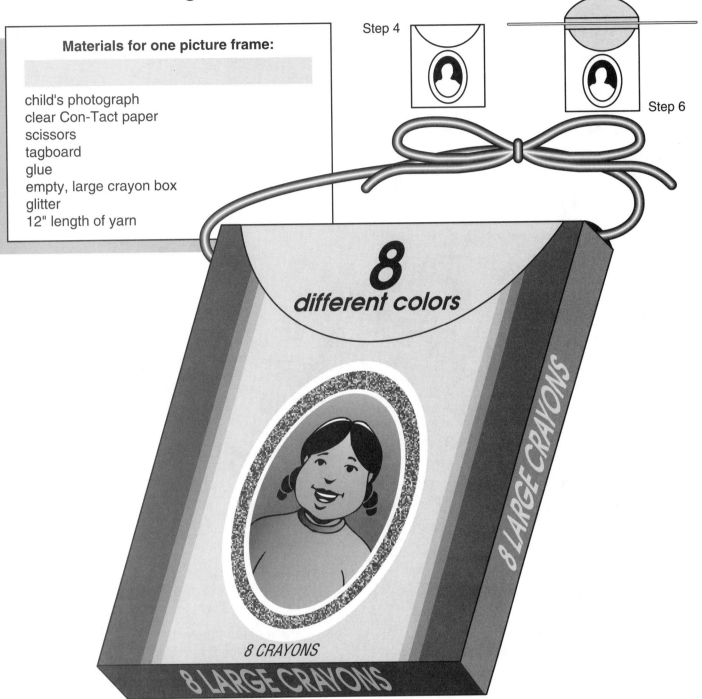

Step 4

Step 6

8
*different colors*

8 LARGE CRAYONS

8 CRAYONS

8 LARGE CRAYONS

**Steps:**

1. Cover the child's photo with clear Con-Tact paper and trim the excess.
2. Cut a tagboard oval that is slightly larger than the photo.
3. Glue the photo to the center of the tagboard oval.
4. Glue the tagboard to the front of the crayon box (Step 4).

5. Squeeze a trail of glue along the edge of the tagboard around the photo. Sprinkle glitter on the glue and shake off the excess glitter. Let the glue dry.
6. Open the crayon box and glue the length of yarn to the inside of the flap as shown (Step 6).
7. Glue the box shut and tie the yarn into a bow for suspending the picture frame.

*Jackie Elmer—Gr. Pre-K,*
*First Presbyterian Preschool, Naples, FL*

# Flowery Heart Wall Hanging

**Materials for one project:**

**pattern on page 77**

9" x 13" piece of lightweight tagboard
glue
9" x 13" piece of wallpaper
scissors
8" length of ribbon or lace
2" length of ribbon
small dried flowers (such as baby's breath)

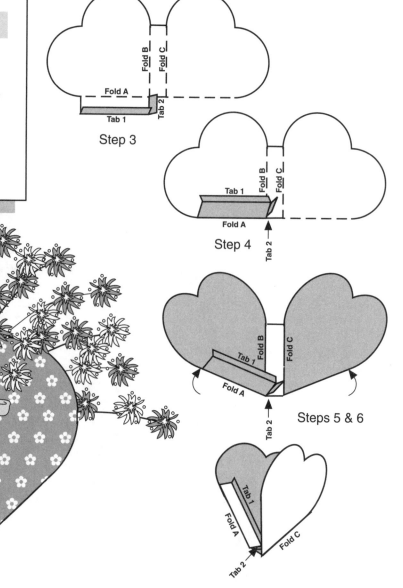

Step 3

Step 4

Steps 5 & 6

**Steps:**

1. Duplicate the pattern on page 77 onto tagboard. Spread a coat of glue over the blank side of the tagboard. Lay the piece of wallpaper faceup atop the tagboard. Align the edges and press gently to smooth the surface. Let the glue dry.
2. Flip over the tagboard. Cut out the pattern on the bold lines.
3. Fold up and crease Tabs 1 and 2 as shown (Step 3).
4. Fold and crease Fold A toward the heart (Step 4).
5. Make a heart-shaped box by folding and creasing Folds B and C toward one another as shown (Steps 5 and 6).
6. Secure the edges of the box by gluing Tabs 1 and 2 to the insides of the box.
7. Tie the eight-inch piece of ribbon or lace into a bow, and glue the bow to the front of the heart-shaped box.
8. Using the two-inch length of ribbon, glue a small loop to the back of the box for suspending it.
9. Fill the box with an arrangement of dried flowers.

*Elaine Svec—Grs. 3–4, Billings Christian School, Billings, MT*

**Pattern**

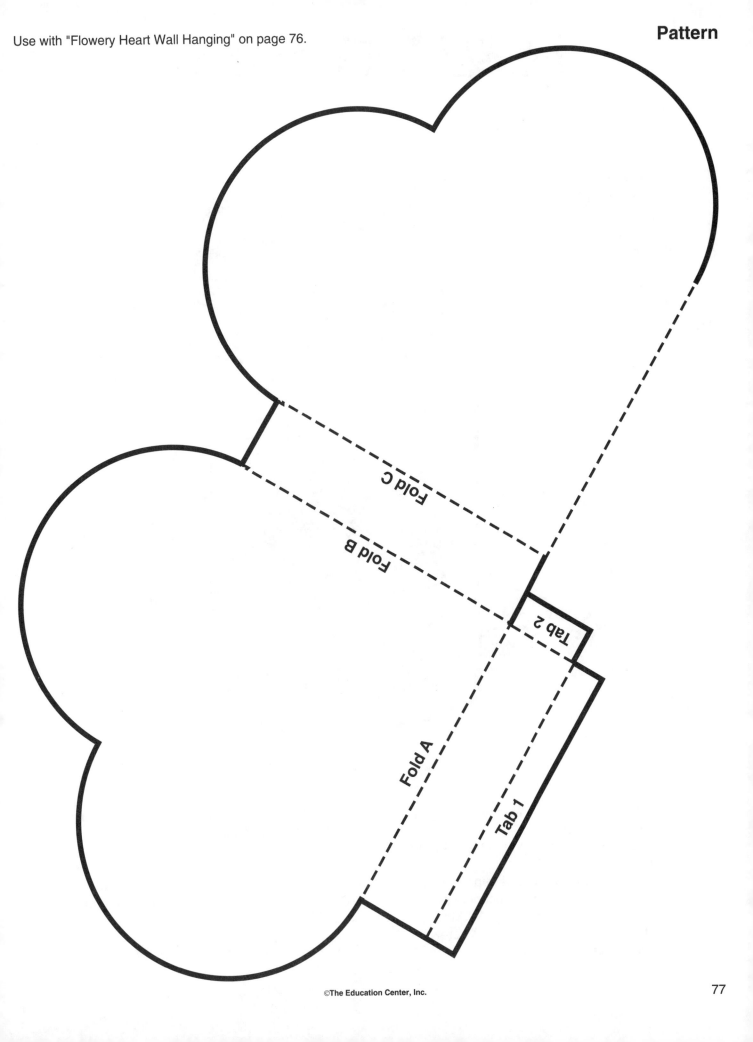

Fold C

Fold B

Tab 2

Fold A

Tab 1

# M&M Gift Jar

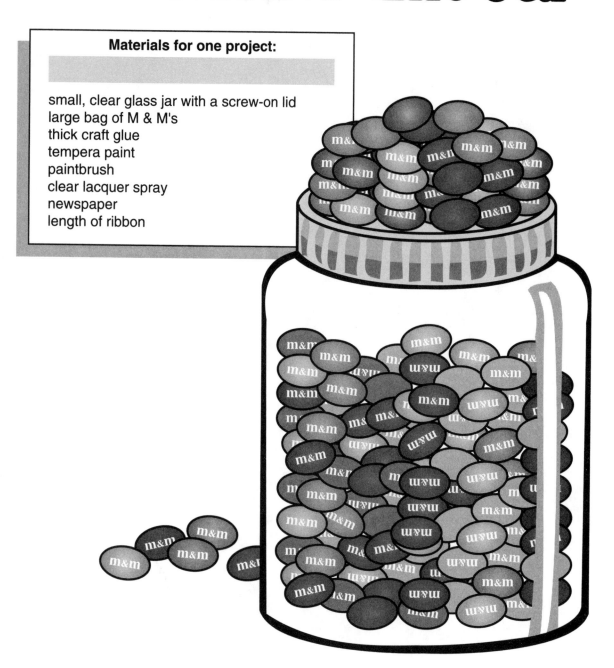

**Materials for one project:**

small, clear glass jar with a screw-on lid
large bag of M & M's
thick craft glue
tempera paint
paintbrush
clear lacquer spray
newspaper
length of ribbon

**Steps:**

1. Use tempera paint to paint the lid of the jar. Allow the lid to dry.
2. Using thick craft glue, mound M&M's atop the lid. Let the glue dry.
3. Cover your tabletop with newspaper. Then spray a thick coat of clear lacquer spray onto the lid and the mound of M&M's.
4. Fill the jar with more M&M's and screw on the M&M-decorated lid.
5. Tie the length of ribbon around the jar to add the finishing touch.

This jar may be used to hold a variety of items. It is important for children to understand that the M&M's on the lid are only for decoration and should not be eaten.

*Betty Lynn Scholtz—Gr. K, St. Ann's School, Charlotte, NC*

# Photo Magnet

**Materials for one project:**

child's photo
12-ounce metal juice-can lid
pencil
scissors
glue
8" length of lace
magnetic tape

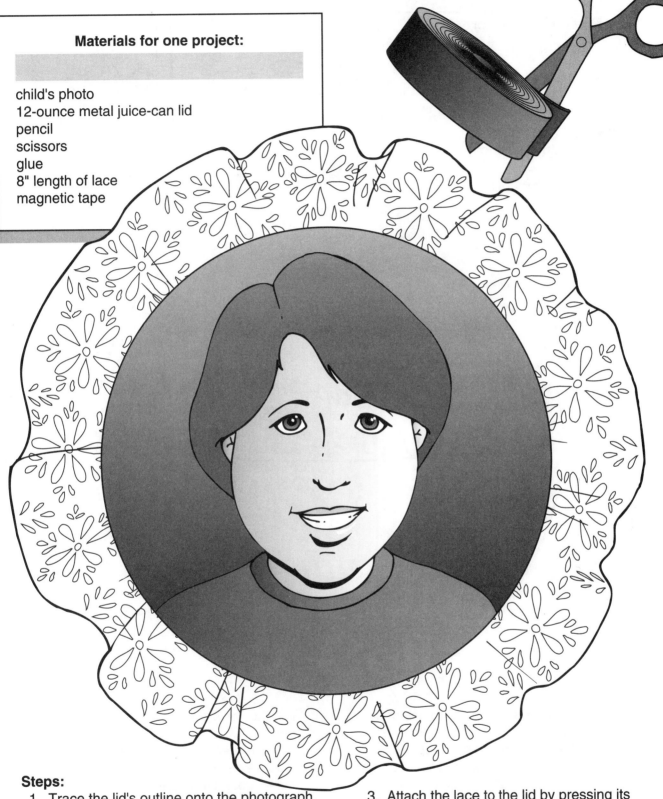

**Steps:**

1. Trace the lid's outline onto the photograph, centering the face within the outline. Cut inside the line; set the photo aside.

2. Squeeze a trail of glue along the groove of the lid; allow the glue to dry just until it is tacky.

3. Attach the lace to the lid by pressing its edge to the glue.

4. Glue the child's photo to the center of the lid.

5. Attach a strip of magnetic tape to the back of the lid.

*Bonnie jo Kyles—Gr. 2, Ennis Elementary, Ennis, MT*

# Mother's Day Note Holder

**Materials for one project:**

two 9" paper plates
glue
hole puncher
1 loop of yarn
1 yellow Styrofoam egg carton
scissors
4 sections from a green Styrofoam egg carton

Step 1

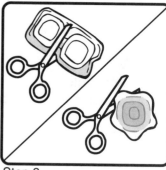

Step 3

*Happy Mother's Day!*

**Steps:**

1. To make the note holder, position one paper plate on a tabletop. Cut the other paper plate in half and invert one half atop the first paper plate. Align the outer edges of the plates and glue them together (Step 1).

2. Using the hole puncher, punch a hole at the top of the holder. Attach the loop of yarn for suspending the holder.

3. Cut apart the sections of the yellow egg carton. Scallop the edges of the sections to make flowers (Step 3).

4. Glue the flowers along the holder's outer edge.

5. From the green egg-carton sections, cut small leaves and glue them in various places around the flowers.

Make a Mother's Day card to go inside the note holder and the gift is ready for delivery.

*Phyllis H. Pettit—Gr. 4, North Chatham Elementary, Chapel Hill, NC*

# Mother's Day Corsage

**Materials for one corsage:**

4" circle tagboard pattern     hot glue gun
pencil
scissors
tissue paper
6" length of yarn
small round doily
tape
narrow ribbon
safety pin

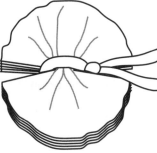

Step 2           Step 3

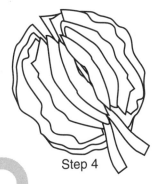

Step 4

Step 6

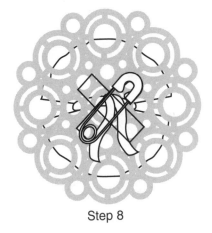

Step 8

## Steps:

1. Use the pattern to trace and cut out six 4-inch circles from tissue paper.
2. Stack the tissue-paper circles and cut a slit on both sides of the stack (Step 2).
3. Gather the tissue by inserting a length of yarn through the slits, gently pulling the yarn, and tying it in a knot (Step 3).
4. Gently separate and twist the layers of tissue paper into a flower shape (Step 4).
5. Make a small hole in the center of the doily.
6. Attach the tissue-paper flower to the doily by inserting the yarn ends through the hole and securing them on the back with tape. Trim the excess yarn. (Step 6)

*(Steps 7 and 8 should be done by an adult.)*

7. Tie the length of ribbon into a bow. Using the hot glue gun, glue the bow onto the front of the doily.
8. Glue a safety pin to the back of the doily with the hot glue gun (Step 8).

*Lisa Lowry—Gr. 1, William M. Anderson School, Dallas, TX*

81

# Mother's Day Fan

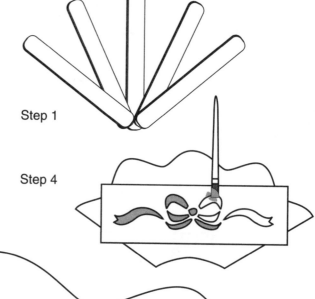

Step 1

Step 4

**Steps:**

1. Glue the five tongue depressors into a fan shape as shown in Step 1. (This step should be done by an adult.)
2. Paint these blades of the fan using tempera paint. Allow the paint to dry.
3. Using the pattern on page 83, cut out a fan shape from plain wallpaper (or heavy textured paper).
4. Make a design on the fan cutout using stencils and tempera paint. Let it dry. (Step 4)
5. Glue the fan cutout to the blades.
6. Tie the length of ribbon into a bow and glue the bow to the front of the fan using a hot glue gun. (This step should be done by an adult.)

*Bonnie Dentler—Gr. Pre-K,*
*Westbrook Park Nursery School, Canton, OH*

**fan**

# Father's Day Paperweight

**Materials for one paperweight:**

2" square of paper       laminating film
scissors       water
small photograph of the child       glitter
glue       sequins
crayons       hot glue gun
baby food jar with a lid
tempera paint
paintbrush
clear lacquer spray

Step 7

**Steps:**

1. Cut a heart from the two-inch square of paper.
2. Glue the photograph to one side of the heart. Color the opposite side with a crayon. Write a message on the heart such as "I love you" or "Happy Father's Day" if desired.
3. Paint the lid of the baby food jar and allow it to dry. Spray the outside of the lid with a coat of clear lacquer. Allow the lacquer to dry completely.
4. Laminate the heart and trim along its outer edge, leaving a slight border of lamination.
5. Place the heart inside the baby food jar and fill the jar to the top with water.
6. Add some glitter and sequins to the water.
7. With the help of another adult, use a hot glue gun to squeeze a trail of glue along the lid's inside edge (Step 7). Press the lid in place on the baby food jar.
8. Shake the jar gently to create a sparkling, swirling Father's Day surprise.

*Jennifer Milo—Gr. K, St. Anthony's School, Schenectady, NY*

# Stuffed Dinosaur

**Materials for one dinosaur:**

**pattern on page 86 or 87**

colored bulletin-board paper    paintbrush
pencil                          markers
scissors
stapler
paper clips (optional for cutting out the
    dinosaurs)
newspaper
tissue-paper shapes (assorted colors)
diluted glue

Step 3

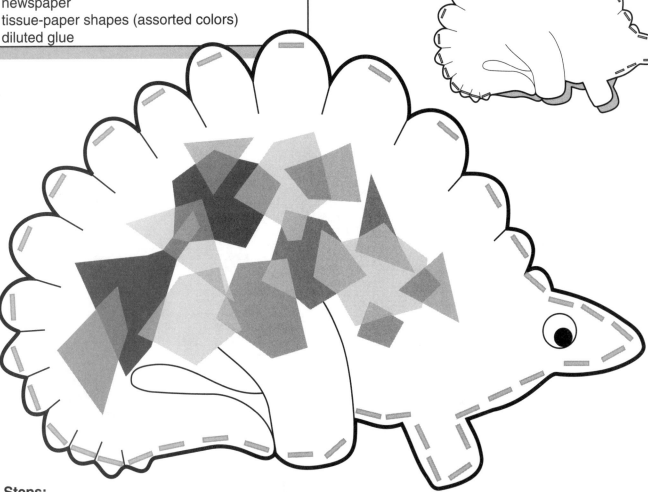

**Steps:**

1. Using an opaque projector, enlarge one of the dinosaur patterns on page 86 or 87 on bulletin-board paper.
2. Staple or paper clip this bulletin-board paper atop a second piece of bulletin-board paper, and cut out two dinosaurs of the same shape.
3. Align the edges of the dinosaurs and staple along the outer edges, leaving a four-inch opening at the bottom (Step 3).

4. Set the project atop newspaper and use diluted glue and a paintbrush to cover both sides of the dinosaur with tissue-paper shapes. Let the glue dry.
5. Stuff the dinosaur with crumpled newspaper; then staple the opening closed.
6. If desired, add other facial features and details to the dinosaur with markers.

*Evelyn J. Hollan—Gr. Pre-K, Merryhill Country Schools, Sacramento, CA*

with "Stuffed Dinosaur" on page 85.

**Pattern**

**Tyrannosaurus Rex**

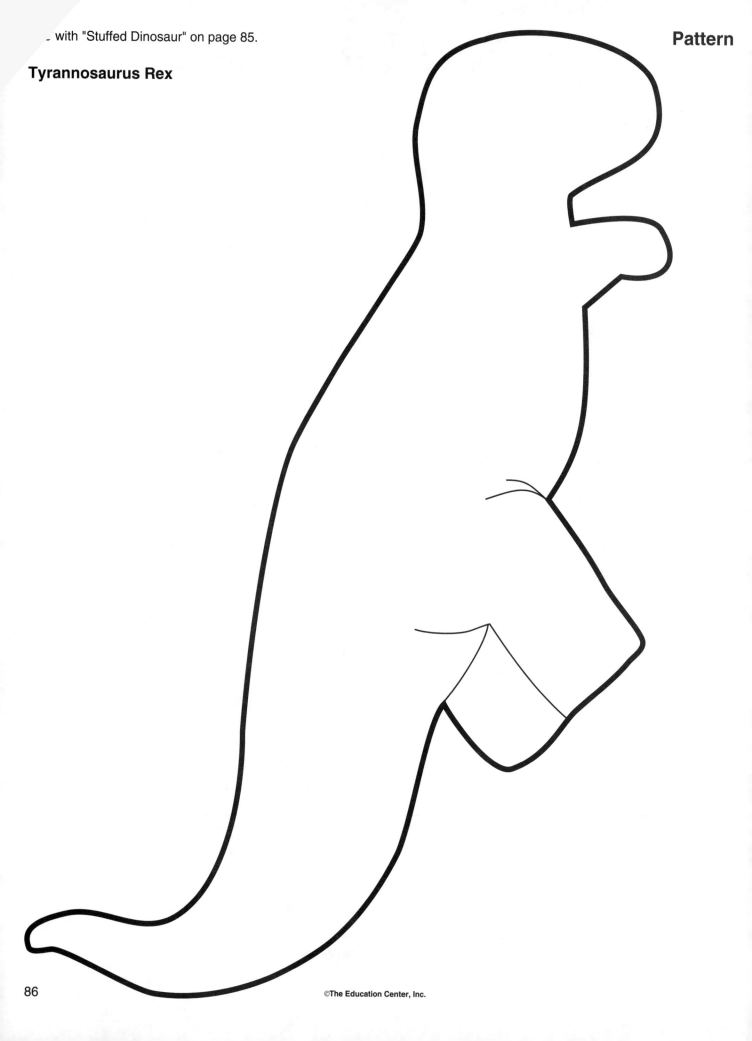

Use with "Stuffed Dinosaur" on page 85.

**Stegosaurus**

# An Underground View

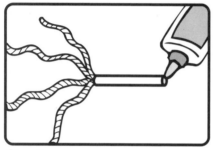

Step 3

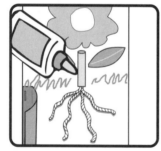

Step 4

**Steps:**

1. Position the white construction paper vertically.
2. Lay the brown construction-paper strip atop the white construction paper, aligning the bottom and side edges. Staple the left edges together to form a flap.
3. Insert one end of the lengths of yarn into the drinking straw so that the yarn hangs from the bottom of the straw. Squeeze a small amount of glue into the end of the straw to secure the ends of the yarn inside. (Step 3)
4. Glue the straw vertically to the white construction paper just above the brown flap as shown in Step 4.
5. Glue the green construction-paper strip atop the drinking straw to form a stem. Hold the paper in place until the glue sets. Secure the edges of the green strip with transparent tape if needed.
6. Spread out and glue the lengths of yarn to the white construction paper (underneath the flap) to create roots.
7. Using construction-paper scraps, scissors, glue, and markers, design a flower around the top of the drinking-straw stem. Let the glue dry.
8. When the flower is complete, open the flap as desired to reveal the plant's root system.

*Susan A. Schneider—Gr. 1, Alpine School, Sparta, NJ*

# Rummage Robots

**Materials:**

an assortment of discarded items (such as milk
   jugs, 2-liter plastic bottles, boxes, buttons,
   yarn, bottle caps, paper-towel rolls, and egg
   cartons)
scissors                     construction paper
glue
tape
markers

*Have your students rummage through their
homes for discarded items to be used in this
recycled project.*

**Steps:**
1. To make one robot, choose a large item
   (such as a milk jug or a two-liter plastic
   bottle) to use for the body.
2. Choose a variety of smaller items to make
   parts such as arms and legs for the robot.
   (Encourage each student to imagine unique
   tasks that his robot could perform to help
   him decide on necessary body parts.)

3. Attach these body parts to the body with
   glue or tape. Decorate your robot with
   markers and construction paper.
4. Give your robot a name and put a name
   label on it.

Try this activity with cooperative-learning groups.
Have each group present its robot to the class
and explain the robot's functions and abilities.

*Carol Ross—Grs. 1–5, Wyland Elementary, St. Louis, MO*

# Recycled Totem Pole

**Steps:**

1. Cut a strip of black construction paper to fit the coffee can.
2. Spread a coat of glue on the coffee can and glue the black construction paper to it. Hold the paper in place until it is secure.
3. Cut out totem pole facial features, shapes, and designs from construction paper, and glue them onto the coffee can. Let the glue dry.

Stack your students' completed projects atop one another to form a class totem pole.

*Mary Manna—Gr. 3, Hedwig Elementary, Elizabeth, NJ*

# Junk Spacecraft

**Materials:**

an assortment of discarded materials (such as
boxes, plastic bottles and jugs, pie pans,
paper cups, medicine cups, paper towel rolls,
and plastic margarine containers)
hot glue gun
construction-paper scraps · glue
cardboard scraps · tempera paints
scissors · paintbrush
length of clear fishing line

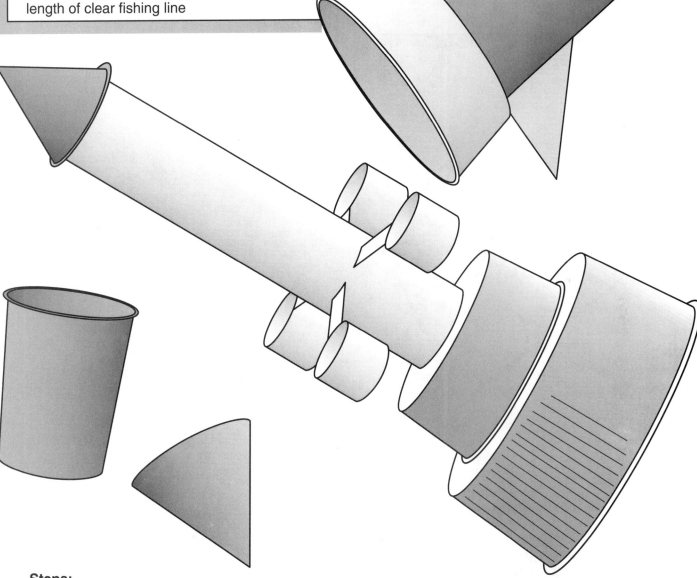

**Steps:**

1. Using an assortment of discarded materials,
   design the body of a spacecraft. Use a hot
   glue gun to glue the items together. (This
   should be done by an adult.)
2. Add details to the spacecraft by cutting and
   gluing on cardboard and construction-paper
   scraps. Let the glue dry.

3. Paint the completed spacecraft as desired.
4. Suspend the spacecraft from the ceiling with
   a length of clear fishing line.

*Bonne Hutton—Art Teacher, North Rock Creek School,
Shawnee, OK*

# Jewelry From Junk

**Materials:**

small cardboard shapes (such as diamonds,
  hearts, and triangles)
glue
an assortment of small objects (such as
  macaroni, buttons, lace, and glitter)
hot glue gun
safety pins

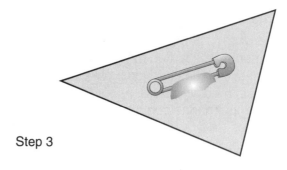

Step 3

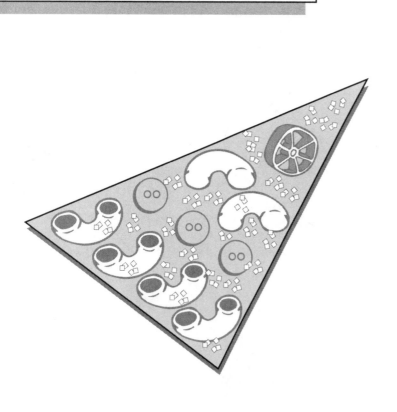

**Steps:**
1. Choose a cardboard shape.
2. Arrange small objects on it. Then glue the
   arrangement in place. Allow the glue to dry.

3. Using a hot glue gun, attach a safety pin to
   the back of the cardboard (Step 3). (This
   step should be done by an adult.)

Your students can wear their homemade pins or
give them as gifts.

*Suzanne Fosburgh—Preschool,*
*De Pere Coop Nursery School, De Pere, WI*

# Recycled Volleyball Net

### Materials for one volleyball net:

40 plastic six-pack rings
162 twist ties
two 5' wooden sticks
sixteen 12" lengths of heavy string

*It's all fun and games with this environmentally smart class activity. Have your students collect plastic six-pack rings and twist ties, and they'll be ready to assemble this project.*

Step 3

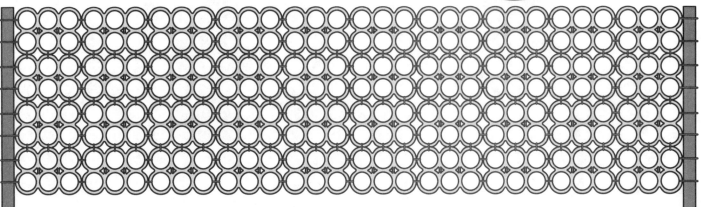

**Steps:**

1. Position the six-pack rings horizontally in four rows of ten rings each.
2. Attach each section to an adjacent section with a twist tie.

3. When the net is complete, tie the strings to the end sections of the net as shown (Step 3). Then tie the net to the five-foot sticks.

*Leda M. Eannace—Gr. K, Saint Bonaventure, Glenshaw, PA*

# Hug The Earth

**Materials for one project:**

**earth pattern on page 95**

white duplicating paper
scissors
crayons
9" paper plate
glue
two 12" x 3" strips of yellow construction paper
hand pattern below
construction paper (assorted skin colors)
pencil

**Pattern**

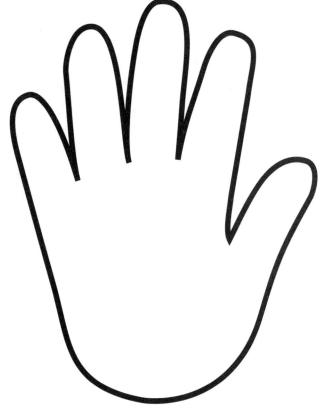

Step 6

**Steps:**

1. Duplicate a copy of the earth pattern on page 95. Cut out the earth outline.
2. Color the earth cutout and glue it to the center of the paper plate.
3. Glue the ends of the yellow strips to the back of the paper plate for arms.
4. Using the hand pattern shown, trace two hands onto construction paper in a desired skin color. Cut out the resulting outlines.
5. Glue the hands in place at the ends of the yellow strips.
6. Glue the arms together as shown in Step 6.

*Jayne M. Gammons—Gr. K, Oak Grove Elementary, Durham, NC*

**earth**

# Ocean Bulletin Board

**Materials:**

aluminum foil
stapler
several sheets of pastel crepe paper
scissors
fishnet

*Set the stage for an ocean unit with this magnificent marine bulletin board.*

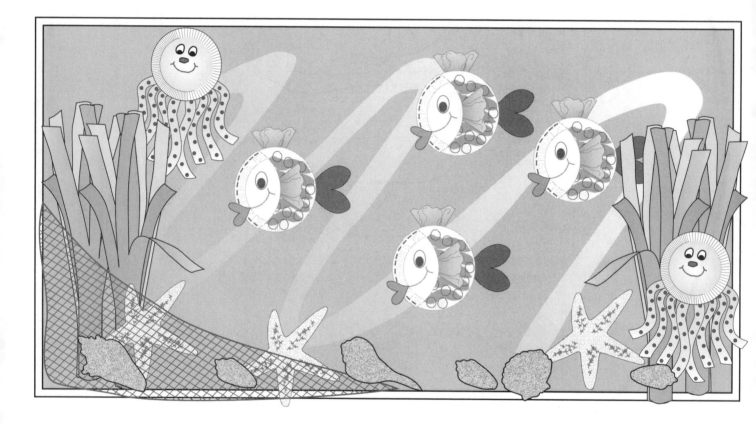

**Steps:**

1. Create a background on your bulletin board by stapling sheets of aluminum foil to cover the board.

2. Cut crepe-paper sheets in varying sizes. Roll up the crepe paper lengthwise to create seaweed. Staple the end of each seaweed length to the bulletin board.

3. Mount a fishnet on a portion of the bulletin board for an added touch.

Have your students make some of the ocean creature art projects detailed in this section of the book to add to your underwater display.

*Jennifer Strathdee—Gr. Pre-K, Parkside School, Solvay, NY*

# Sensational Seashells

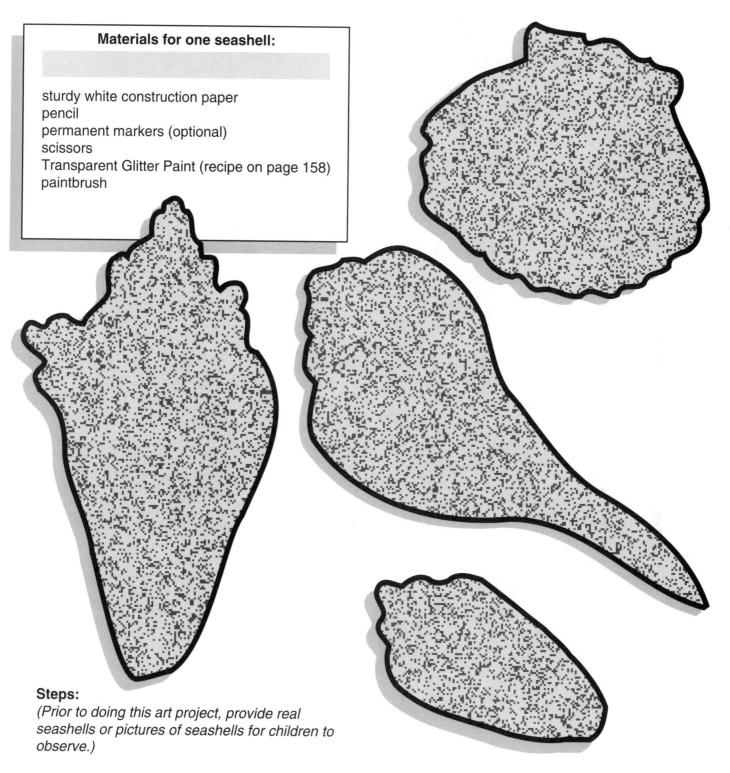

**Materials for one seashell:**

sturdy white construction paper
pencil
permanent markers (optional)
scissors
Transparent Glitter Paint (recipe on page 158)
paintbrush

**Steps:**
*(Prior to doing this art project, provide real seashells or pictures of seashells for children to observe.)*

1. Choose a seashell and draw its shape on white construction paper. If desired, use permanent markers before painting to add details to the shell.

2. Cut out the seashell shape.
3. Using a paintbrush, brush on a coat of Transparent Glitter Paint. Let the paint dry before displaying the shell.

*Jennifer Strathdee—Gr. Pre-K, Parkside School, Solvay, NY*

# Textured Starfish

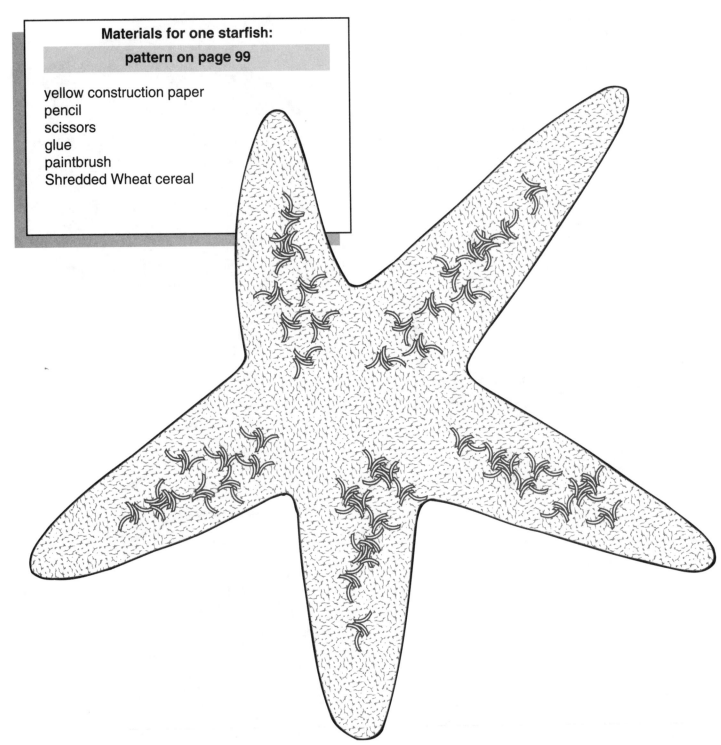

**Materials for one starfish:**

**pattern on page 99**

yellow construction paper
pencil
scissors
glue
paintbrush
Shredded Wheat cereal

**Steps:**

1. Using the pattern on page 99, trace or duplicate a starfish onto yellow construction paper. Cut on the resulting outline.
2. Using a paintbrush, brush a coat of glue on the surface of the starfish.
3. Crumble Shredded Wheat and sprinkle it evenly on the starfish to give the creature a realistic look.

*Tammy Stapley—Gr. Pre-K, Little Lambs Preschool, Yuba City, CA*

Use with "Textured Starfish" on page 98.

**starfish**

# Stuffed Aquatic Creatures

## Materials:

bulletin-board paper (assorted colors)
pencil
scissors
glue
hole puncher
plastic produce bags (recycled)
long, narrow tissue-paper strips (for jellyfish)

Step 2

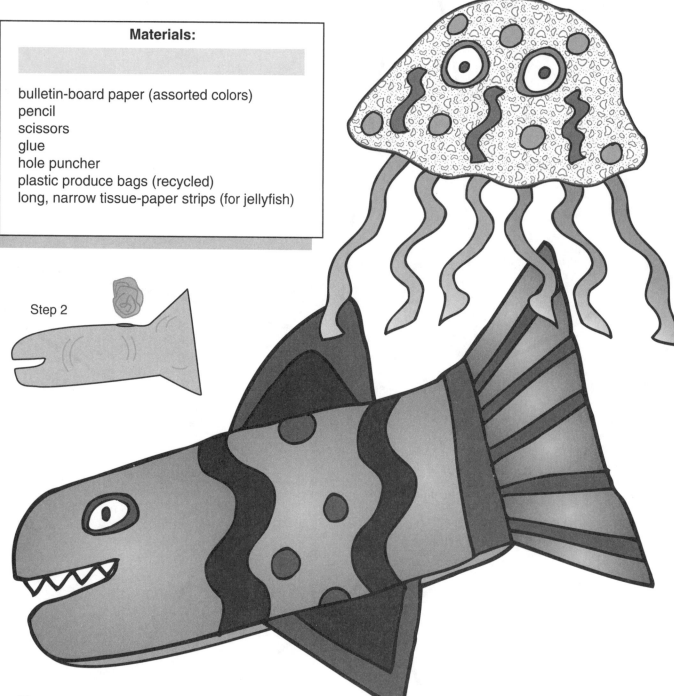

## Steps:

1. Stack two large pieces of bulletin-board paper. Draw and cut out the front and back of an ocean creature.
2. Glue the edges of the two outlines together, leaving a three-inch opening for stuffing the creature (Step 2).
3. Use bulletin-board paper cutouts (cut from the scraps) to decorate both sides of the creature. (Use a hole puncher to punch assorted colors of dots to glue on the creature, if desired.) Let the glue dry.
4. Stuff the creature with plastic bags. Then glue the open edges closed.

If a student chooses to make a jellyfish, have him crumple tissue-paper strips to use for tentacles.

*Polly Lockhart—Gr. 4, Madison Park School, Woodward, OK*

# No Ordinary Octopus

9" white paper plate
8 lengths of white crepe-paper streamers
glue
red self-adhesive dots (approximately 60)
markers (various colors)

Step 1

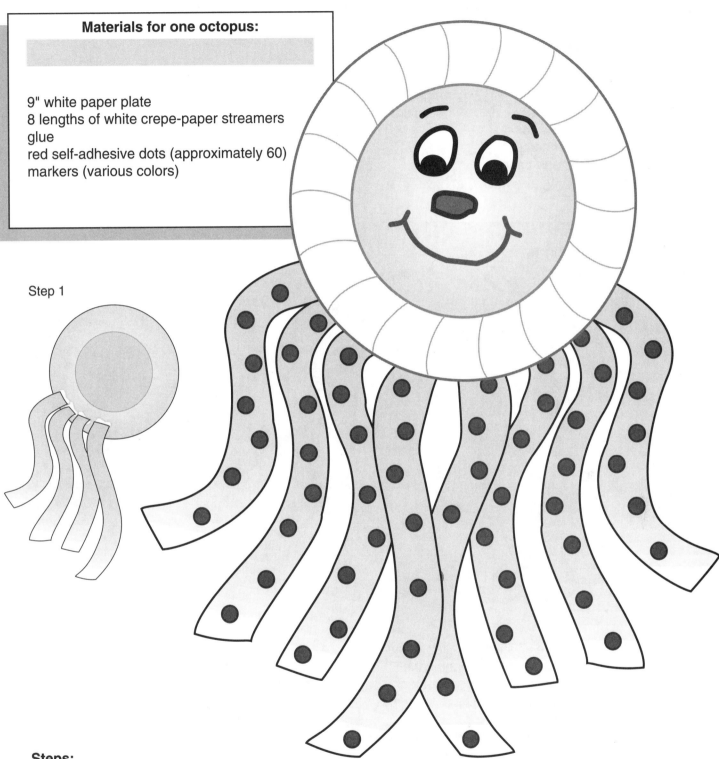

**Steps:**

1. To make the body of the octopus, invert the paper plate; then glue the ends of the streamers, side by side, to the back side of the plate (Step 1).
2. Turn the octopus over. Using various colors of markers, draw facial features and other desired details on the paper plate.
3. Attach several red self-adhesive dots to each streamer for the octopus's suckers.

Suspend these cute creatures from your ceiling with string or display them on an ocean bulletin board.

*Kristy Osborn, Ball State University, Muncie, IN*

# Fancy Fish

### Materials for one fish:

#### patterns on page103

two 9" paper plates
stapler
colored chalk
crepe paper (various colors)
construction-paper scraps
blue and green crepe-paper
  streamers

glue
string
scissors

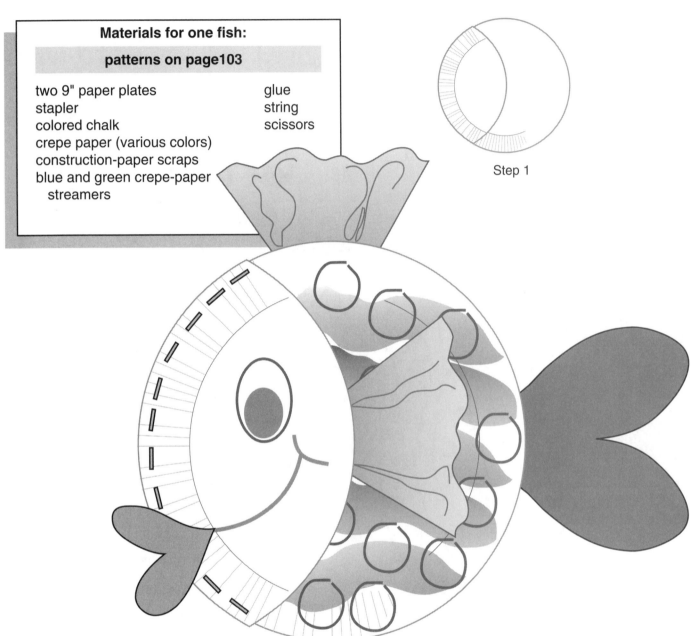

Step 1

## Steps:

1. Cut a paper plate as shown in Step 1 and invert it atop another plate, aligning the outer edges. Staple the plates together along the edges to form the fish's body and gill.
2. Color the body of the fish with two complementary chalk colors, and use your fingers to blend the chalk.
3. Using the patterns on page 103, cut two fins and a tail from crepe paper.
4. Gently stretch the curved edge of each fin piece to make a wavy edge. Glue the point of one fin to the top of the fish. Glue the other fin to the side of the fish and attach the tail to the back of the fish.
5. Add eyes, a mouth, and other details to the fish with chalk or construction-paper cutouts.

With a length of string, suspend the fish from the ceiling amidst a sea of blue and green crepe-paper streamers.

*Katherine E. Gegner—Gr. 2, W. M. Bass School, Lynchburg, VA*

Use with "Fancy Fish" on page 102.

fin

tail

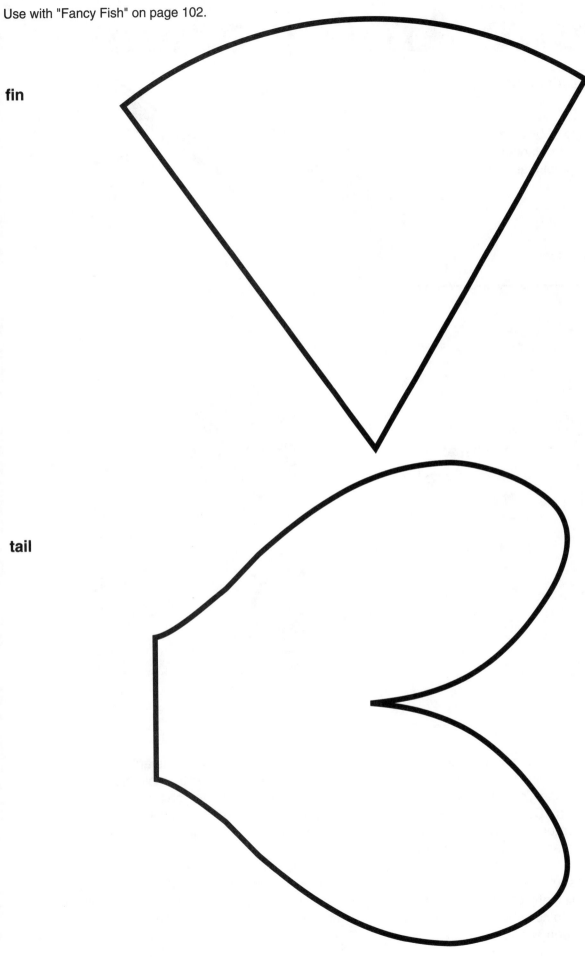

# Quite An Aquarium

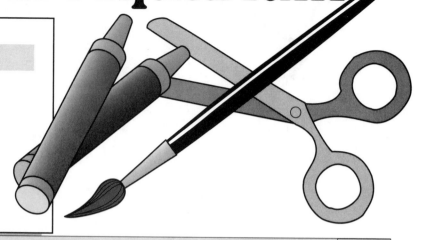

**Materials for one aquarium:**

12" x 18" rectangle of blue cellophane
two 1½" x 12" strips of tagboard
two 1½" x 18" strips of tagboard
glue
tempera paints
paintbrush
scissors
white construction paper
crayons

**Steps:**

1. Position the cellophane horizontally.
2. Border the cellophane with tagboard strips by gluing the strips along the cellophane edges as shown. (Be sure to overlap the strips in the corners for sturdiness.)
3. Paint the strips as desired. Allow the paint to dry.
4. On white construction paper, use crayons to color fish, snails, and other marine animals. (It is important to color heavily so the creatures can be seen easily.)
5. Cut out the colored marine animals. Spread a thin coat of glue on the colored side of each animal; then attach the animals to the back side of the aquarium in a desired arrangement. (The glue will dry clear.)

For added flair, border both sides of the cellophane with tagboard strips and color both sides of the animals. Then display your aquariums in windows and watch the sun illuminate your underwater creations!

104

*Virginia M. O'Connor, St. Raphael School, Medford, MA*

# Fishbowl Fanfare

**Materials for one project:**

**fishbowl pattern on page 106**

construction paper (light blue, orange,
  and green)
scissors
crayons
glue
dried beans (any kind)

**Steps:**

1. Using the pattern on page 106, trace or duplicate the fishbowl onto light blue construction paper.
2. Draw three fish of any kind on orange construction paper and cut them out. If desired, add details to the fish with crayons.
3. Draw water plants on green construction paper and cut them out.
4. Glue the water plants to the fishbowl. Then glue the fish atop the plants.
5. Glue dried beans along the bottom of the fishbowl for stones to complete the project.

Donna Ayers—Gr. 1, Brookview Elementary School, Jacksonville, FL

# Pattern

Use with "Fishbowl Fanfare" on page 105.

**fishbowl**

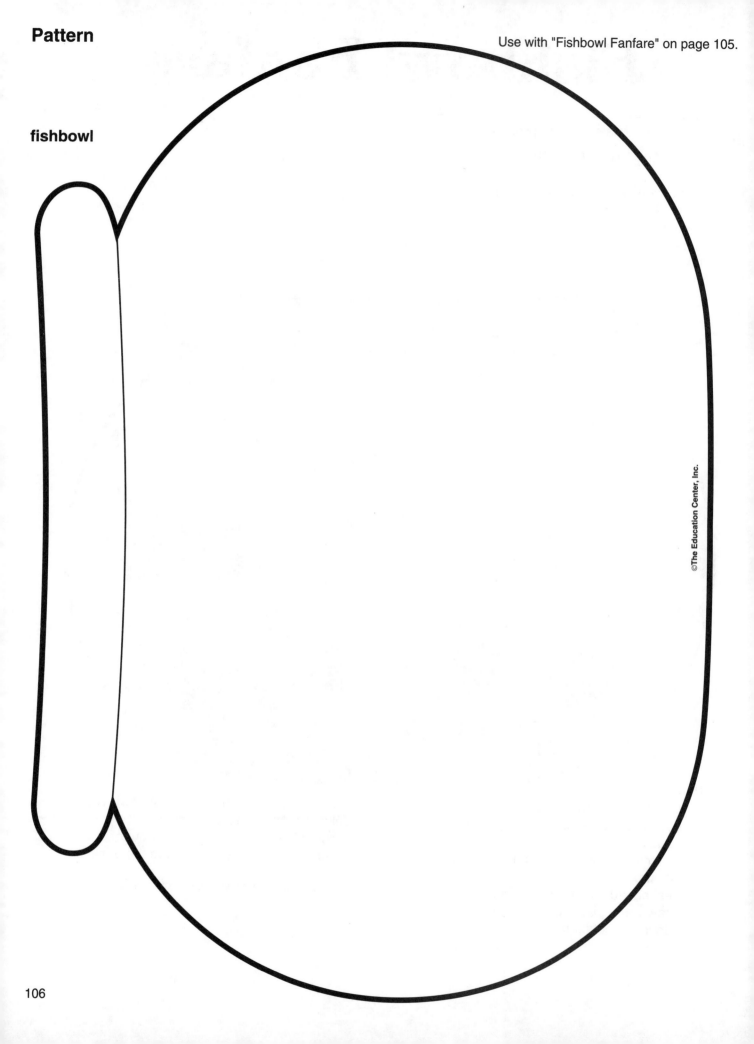

©The Education Center, Inc.

# Mountain Shadows

## Materials for one project:

water
paintbrush
paper towel
purple watercolor paint
9" x 12" construction paper (white, pink,
   light purple, dark purple, and black)
ruler
glue
markers

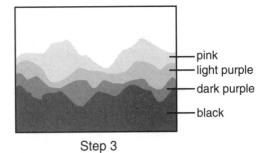

pink
light purple
dark purple
black

Step 3

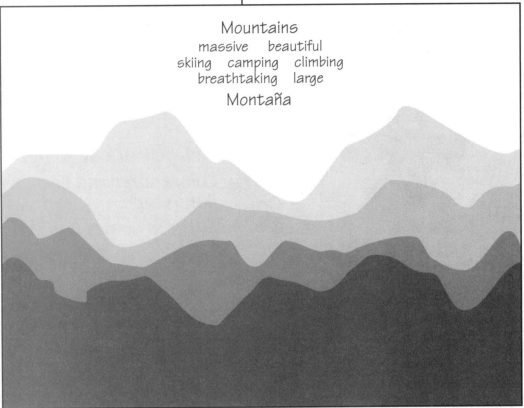

Mountains
massive    beautiful
skiing   camping   climbing
breathtaking   large
Montaña

## Steps:

1. Brush water over the surface of the white construction paper. Then brush the wet surface lightly with purple watercolor. Wipe off the surface immediately with a paper towel, leaving the paper lightly tinted. Allow the paper to dry.

2. From the pink construction paper, tear off a jagged 12-inch strip (approximately three inches wide). Discard the strip and glue the remaining paper atop the tinted paper, aligning the straight edges.

3. With each of the remaining colors of construction paper, tear off approximately one-half inch more from the 12-inch edge each sheet in the following color order: light purple, dark purple, and black. Glue each torn piece of paper atop the previous piece, aligning the straight edges. (Step 3)

4. Complete the project by writing a poem about mountains, sunsets, or shadows at the top of the picture.

*Jane E. Renfrow—Gr. 4, Glacier Gateway Elementary, Columbia Falls, MT*

# Autumn Leaf Haiku

**Materials for one project:**

construction paper or writing paper
scissors
1 sheet of 12" x 18" construction paper
rubber cement
colorful autumn leaves (pressed)
laminating film or clear Con-Tact paper

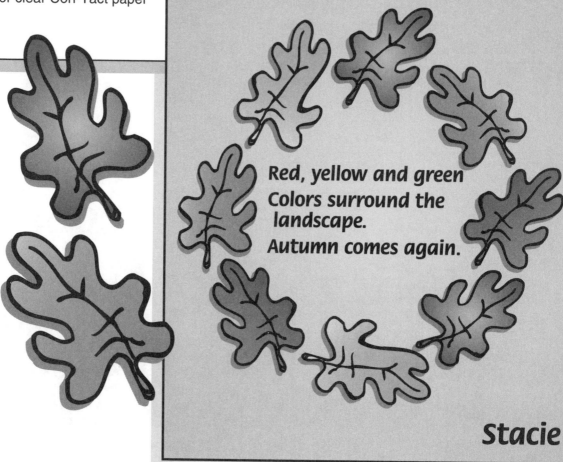

Red, yellow and green
Colors surround the
    landscape.
Autumn comes again.

Stacie

**Steps:**
(Before doing this project, have students write autumn haiku poems.)

1. After writing a haiku poem, copy the poem onto construction paper or writing paper. Cut around the poem, creating a unique shape.
2. Position the 12" x 18" sheet of construction paper vertically. Attach the poem cutout in the center of the paper with rubber cement.
3. Apply rubber cement to the backs of several autumn leaves; then attach the leaves to the construction or writing paper around the poem.
4. Laminate the project or cover it with clear Con-Tact paper.

*Ursula Heinrich—Gr. 4, George Washington School, White Plains, NY*

# Imaginative Adjectives

**Materials:**

discarded magazines
scissors
construction paper (various colors)
rubber cement
black marker

**Steps:**
1. Cut out words from discarded magazines that describe your personality, your appearance, and your hobbies.
2. After finding 25–30 different words, arrange the cutouts on a piece of construction paper in a unique pattern or design.
3. Attach the words to your paper with rubber cement.
4. Use a black marker to add details to your design.

Your students will enjoy creating works of art using descriptive words!

*Karen Ann Perry—Gr. 6, College Station Elementary, College Station, AR*

# Magazine Combination Picture

### Materials:

discarded nature and science magazines
scissors
rubber cement
construction paper (various colors)

Common name: Red-legged hatter
Scientific name: *Rouge hattis*

### Steps:

1. From discarded magazines, cut out animal parts such as legs, tails, and heads from a variety of animals.
2. Rubber cement the animal parts together on construction paper to make an unusual creature. If desired, add silly details to your creature such as a hat, a tie, or shoes.
3. When the creature is complete, give the animal a common and a scientific name. Write these names below the picture. Then write a report telling about your animal's habitat, diet, and other interesting details.

Use this silly project to accompany a unit about animal identification.

*Dolores Daniels—Grs. 5 & 6, North Chili Christian School, North Chili, NY*

# State Collage

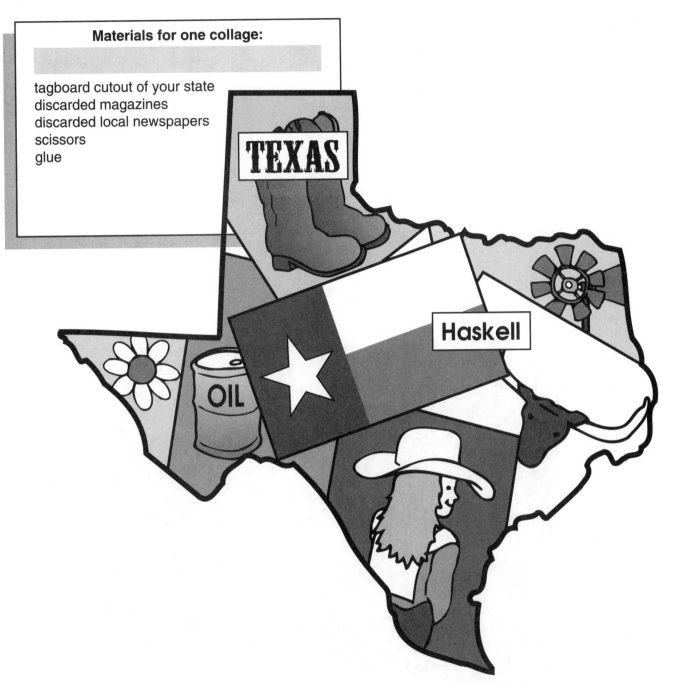

**Materials for one collage:**

tagboard cutout of your state
discarded magazines
discarded local newspapers
scissors
glue

**Steps:**

1. From discarded magazines and newspapers, cut out pictures, names, and other words related to your state (such as state products, points of interest, and famous people).
2. Cut out enough pictures and words to cover the surface of your state cutout.
3. Glue the pictures to your cutout in collage fashion. Trim as needed at the borders.
4. When the collage is complete, locate and cut out the names of your state and city. Glue the state name at the top or center of your collage; then glue your city's name in its general location on the state collage.

This individual or cooperative group project is a terrific way to culminate a unit about your state.

*Lana Stewart—Gr. 2, Haskell Elementary, Haskell, TX*

111

# Cursive Writing Slates

Step 1

Step 2

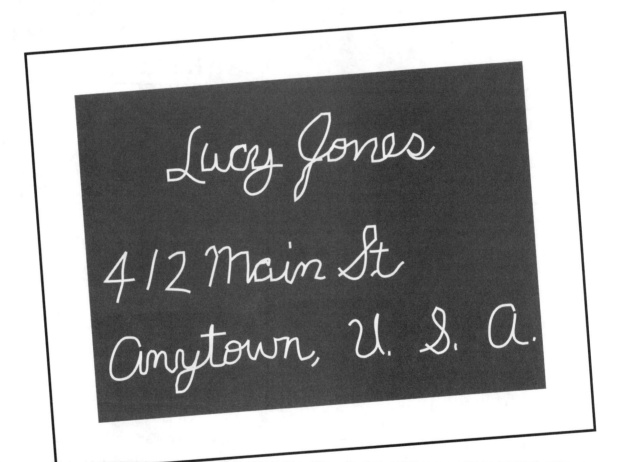

## Steps:

1. Fold a sheet of white construction paper in half. Use a ruler to draw and cut out a half-inch border around the unfolded edges as shown in Step 1.
2. Glue the white border atop the sheet of black construction paper, aligning the edges (Step 2).
3. Using white chalk, write several cursive letters or words on the black paper.
4. Spray the cursive writing with hairspray to set the chalk. Let it dry.
5. Color the frame as desired.

This project is a great way to preserve your students' first cursive writing efforts.

*Pam Williams—Gr. 3, Dixieland Elementary, Lakeland, FL*

# Soap Creatures

### Materials for one soap creature:

one oval-shaped bar of soap
12" square of nylon netting
12" length of ribbon
4 ball-tip straight pins
several plain straight pins
pom-poms (various sizes and colors)

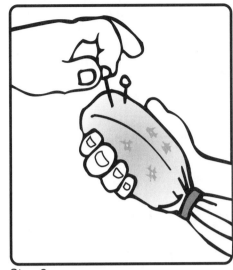

Step 2

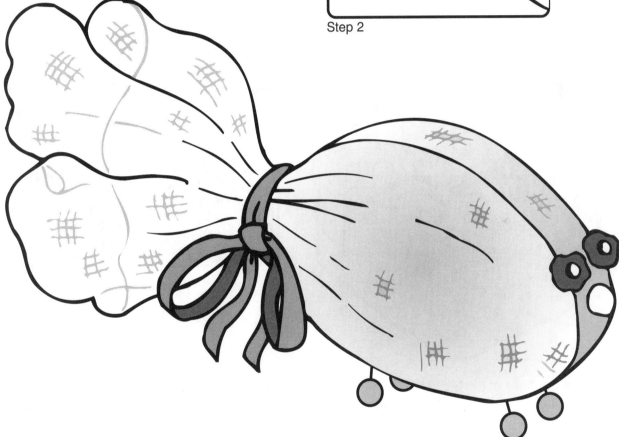

**Steps:**

1. Wrap the nylon netting around the bar of soap. Gather the excess netting and tie it with the length of ribbon.
2. Into the bottom of your bar of soap, push four ball-tip pins for the creature's legs (Step 2).
3. Add eyes, ears, a nose, a mouth, and other features by pushing straight pins through pom-poms in various places on the creature.
4. Display your sweet-smelling creature for all to see.

*Kathryn Kaiser—Gr. K, St. John Vianney School, Orlando, FL*

113

# Wonderful Woven Basket

**Materials for one basket:**

1/2"-wide strips of tagboard
glue
paper clips
scissors
decorative items (such as buttons, lace, or
   ribbon)

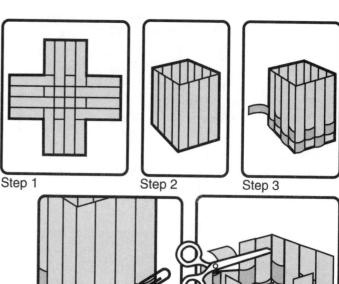

Step 1  Step 2  Step 3

Step 4  Step 5

Step 6  Step 7

## Steps:

1. To form the base of the basket, weave several strips of tagboard as shown in Step 1.

2. When the desired base size is achieved, fold each strip upward as shown in Step 2.

3. To form the sides of the basket, weave strips, one at a time, around the basket as shown. While weaving, crease the strips at the corners. (Step 3)

4. After weaving each level of the basket, trim the strip and glue it in place. Secure the ends with a paper clip until the glue dries. (Step 4)

5. Continue in this manner until the desired height is achieved. Then cut the inside strips even with the top of the basket and secure them with glue. (Step 5)

6. Cut each outside strip a half-inch above the top of the basket. Fold the top of each strip inside the basket and glue it into place. (Step 6)

7. Add a handle by weaving the ends of a strip into the sides of the basket. Glue the ends in place. (Step 7)

8. Glue ribbon, lace, and decorative buttons to the basket to complete the project.

*Ruth Meryweather, Gales Ferry, CT*

# Four-Color Overlay

## Materials for one project:

4 contrasting sheets of 9" x 12" construction
   paper
pencil
scissors
stapler

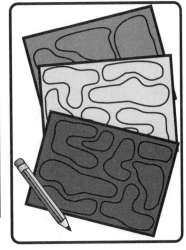

Step 1

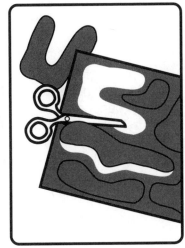

Step 2

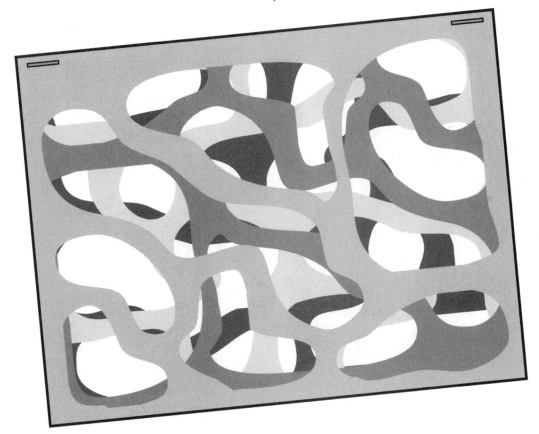

## Steps:

1. On each of three of the sheets of construction paper, use a pencil to draw large, irregular shapes. These shapes should not touch one another, but should be ¼-inch to ½-inch apart. (Step 1)
2. Cut the shapes from each of the three pieces of construction paper. Discard the shapes and keep the paper frames. (Step 2)
3. Stack all four sheets of construction paper with the solid sheet on the bottom. Align the edges of the papers and staple the sheets together at the corners.

*Dolores Daniels—Grs. 5–6, North Chili Christian School, North Chili, NY*

# Patriotic Hat

## Materials for one hat:

9" paper plate
12-ounce paper or plastic bowl
hole puncher
ten 2" strips ⅜"-wide red ribbon
10 gold or silver star stickers
construction paper (blue and white)
star pattern below
two 12" lengths of red yarn

glue
scissors

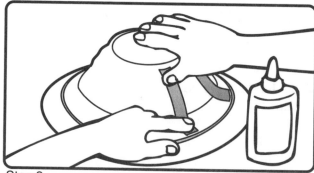

Step 2

Step 4

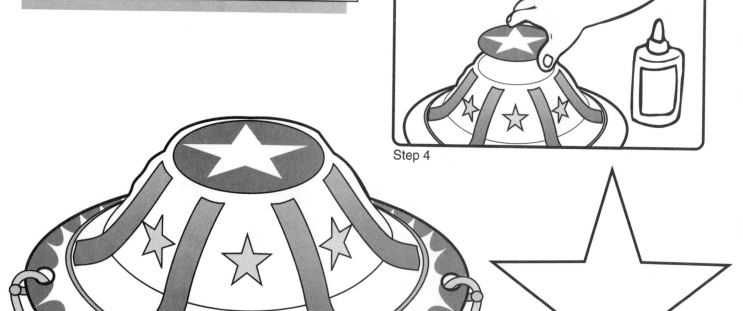

**Pattern**

**Steps:**

1. Invert the paper plate on a tabletop. Invert the bowl on top of the plate and glue it in place.
2. Glue each strip of ribbon from the rim of the bowl to the base as shown in Step 2.
3. Attach the star stickers in the sections between the ribbons.
4. From blue construction paper, cut a circle the size of the bowl's base. Glue the circle in place. (Step 4)
5. Trace the star pattern shown on white construction paper. Cut it out and glue it to the center of the blue circle.
6. Using a hole puncher, punch a hole on either side of the paper plate near the rim.
7. Tie a length of yarn through each hole.

*Clealyn B. Wilson—Gr. 1, East Dover Elementary, Dover, DE*

116

# American Freedom Flag

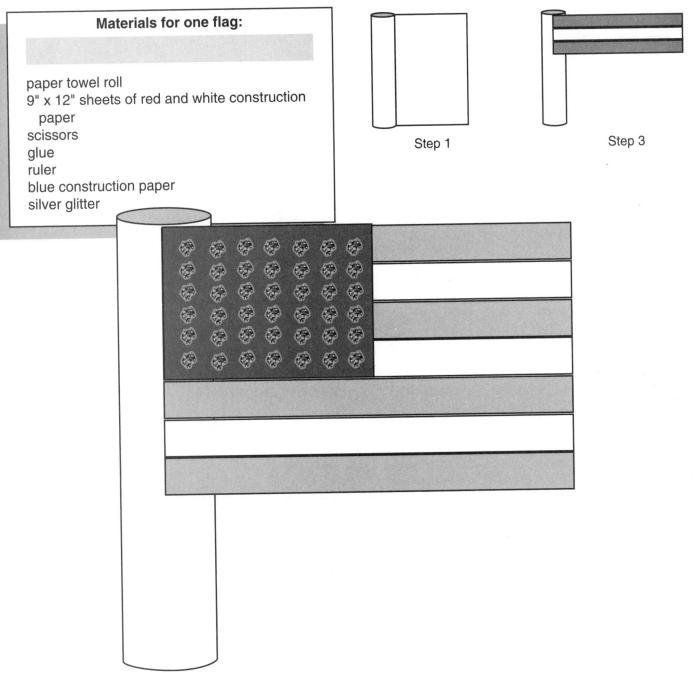

**Materials for one flag:**

paper towel roll
9" x 12" sheets of red and white construction
  paper
scissors
glue
ruler
blue construction paper
silver glitter

Step 1

Step 3

**Steps:**
1. Cover the paper towel roll with white construction paper. Trim the excess paper and secure the loose edges with dabs of glue. (Step 1)
2. Cut four 1" x 12" strips from the red sheet of construction paper and three 1" x 12" strips from the white sheet.
3. Glue the end of each strip to the paper towel roll, alternating colors (Step 3).
4. From blue construction paper, cut a 4 1/2" x 6" rectangle. Glue the rectangle horizontally atop the ends of the first four strips of paper as shown.
5. Place dots of glue on the blue rectangle and sprinkle them with silver glitter. Shake off the excess glitter and allow the flag to dry.

*Clealyn B. Wilson—Gr. 1, East Dover Elementary, Dover, DE*

# Pussy Willow Picture

**Materials for one picture:**

**pattern on page 119**

one sheet of 12" x 18"
  construction paper
assorted colors of
  construction paper
glue
16 cotton swabs
scissors
9" x 12" brown construction paper
pencil

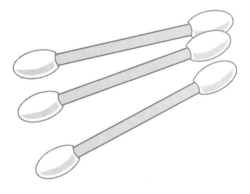

**Steps:**

1. Using the pattern on page 119, trace or duplicate a pussy willow stem onto brown construction paper. Cut on the resulting outline.
2. Design and cut out a vase from a different color of construction paper.
3. Position the 12" x 18" sheet of construction paper vertically on a tabletop, and glue both the stem and the vase to the paper.
4. Cut the ends from 16 cotton swabs. Glue the cotton ends to the stem as shown.

*Kay Gray—Gr. Pre-K, Edwards Road Baptist Church, Greenville, SC*

Use with "Pussy Willow Picture" on page 118.

**pussy willow stem**

# Pink Piggy Bank

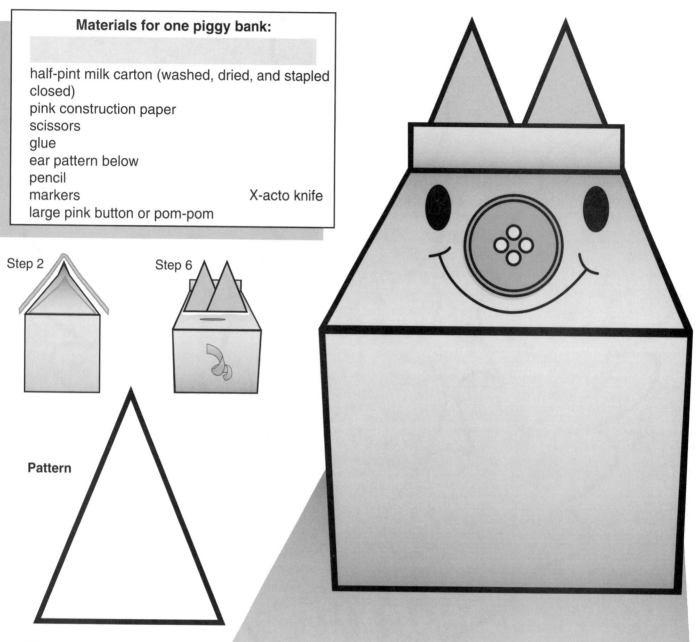

**Materials for one piggy bank:**

half-pint milk carton (washed, dried, and stapled closed)
pink construction paper
scissors
glue
ear pattern below
pencil
markers                                 X-acto knife
large pink button or pom-pom

**Step 2**

**Step 6**

**Pattern**

**Steps:**

1. Cut a strip of pink construction paper to fit around your milk carton. Spread a coat of glue on the sides of the milk carton and wrap the strip of pink construction paper around the sides. Hold the strip in place until the glue is dry.

2. Fold another strip of pink construction paper over the top of the carton and glue the strip in place (Step 2). Let the glue dry.

3. Using the pattern shown, trace the pig's ears on pink construction paper and cut on the resulting outlines. Glue the ears to the back of the milk carton.

4. Cut a small strip of pink construction paper and curl it around a pencil. Then attach it to the back side of the carton for a tail.

5. On the front of the carton, use markers to draw eyes and a mouth. Then glue the button or pom-pom in place for a snout.

6. Using an X-acto knife, cut a quarter-sized slit in the back of the carton as shown in Step 6. (This step should be done by an adult.)

*Kathleen Miller—Gr. K, Our Lady Of Mount Carmel, Tenafly, NJ*

# Grasshoppers Galore

## Materials:

paper egg cartons
thick, green tempera paint
paintbrush
leg and wing patterns shown
construction paper (green, white, and black)
pencil
scissors
glue
hole puncher          green pipe cleaners

**Patterns**

**wings pattern**

**leg pattern**

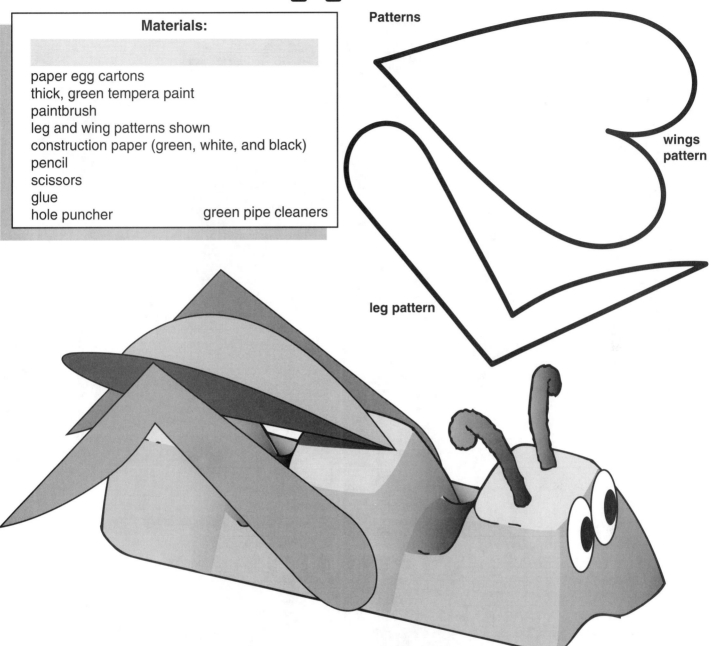

## Steps:

1. Cut a three-segment piece of egg carton for one grasshopper.
2. Paint the egg carton segment with thick, green tempera paint; let it dry.
3. Using the patterns shown, trace the leg twice and the wings once onto green construction paper, and cut on the resulting outlines.
4. Glue a leg to either side of the second segment of the egg carton.
5. Fold the wings in half. Squeeze a trail of glue along the outer edge of the fold. Then glue the wings to the top of the egg carton on the second and third segments.
6. Cut two 1-inch circles from white construction paper. Using a hole puncher, punch two black circles, and glue each one atop a white circle to make eyes.
7. Glue the completed eyes to the front of the first segment.
8. Cut two 2-inch pieces of pipe cleaner for antennae. Press the pipe cleaner pieces into the top of the first segment and curl the ends.

*Julie Ackerman—Gr. Pre-K, Toms River Nursery School, Toms River, NJ*

# Personal Bear Puzzle

**Materials for one puzzle:**

**pattern on page 123**

9" x 12" brown construction paper
pencil
scissors        glitter
tempera paint      glue
paintbrush
colored chalk
crayons
laminating film or clear Con-Tact paper

**Steps:**

1. Using the pattern on page 123, trace the bear on brown construction paper. Cut on the resulting outline.
2. Using tempera paint, colored chalk, and crayons, decorate the bear cutout with clothes and bear facial features. Add a touch of sparkle to the bear by gluing on glitter. Shake off the excess glitter.
3. When the bear is dry, laminate it or cover it with clear Con-Tact paper. Trim along the bear's outer edges to remove the excess lamination.
4. To create a puzzle, cut the bear into four wavy or zigzag pieces.

*Jennifer A. Milo—Gr. K, St. Anthony's School, Schenectady, NY*

Use with "Coffee Grounds Teddy Bear" on page 140
and with "Personal Bear Puzzle" on page 122.

**Pattern**

# Puzzle Apple Tree

## Materials for one tree:

9" x 12" blue construction paper
crayons (brown and assorted colors)
glue
small, discarded puzzle pieces (green on one side)
hole puncher or apple hole puncher
red construction-paper scraps

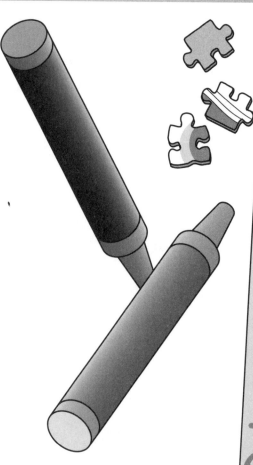

## Steps:

1. On the piece of 9" x 12" blue construction paper, color a tree trunk and branches using a brown crayon.

2. Spread a coat of glue on each of several puzzle pieces and attach them—green side up—to the tree. Continue in this manner until the tree branches are covered with puzzle-piece leaves.

3. Using the hole puncher, punch several holes from red construction paper for apples. Glue the apples in various places on the tree.

4. Complete the picture by adding desired details with crayons.

*Mary Lee Thole—Gr. 1, St. Mary's Public Elementary, Trenton, IL*

# Salt Bottle Creatures

**Materials for one creature:**

small clear bottle (empty)
salt
small plastic containers
food coloring
modeling clay
assorted scraps (such as yarn, fabric, buttons,
    and construction paper)
scissors
glue

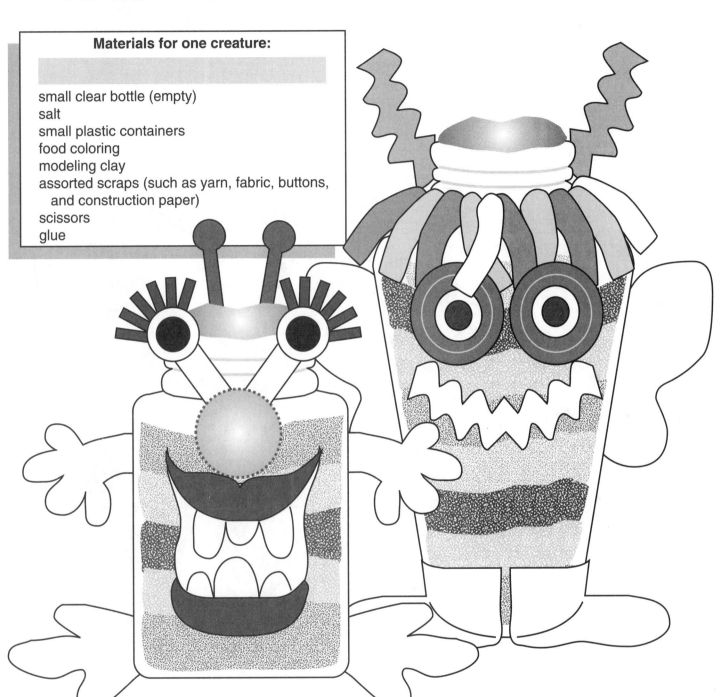

**Steps:**

1. In each of several plastic containers, mix salt with a few drops of food coloring until the desired color is achieved. Let the salt dry.

2. Fill the bottle with various colors of salt, carefully layering the colors as desired.

3. Seal the bottle by pushing a small piece of clay into the opening.

4. Use the assorted scraps to make arms, legs, and facial features for your creature. Glue these pieces to the outside of the bottle.

*Gerrie Gutowski—Gr. 3, Sombra Del Monte School, Albuquerque, NM*

# Window Stickers

**Materials:**

clear plastic material (available in most fabric stores)
pen
coloring books (optional)
fabric paints
scissors

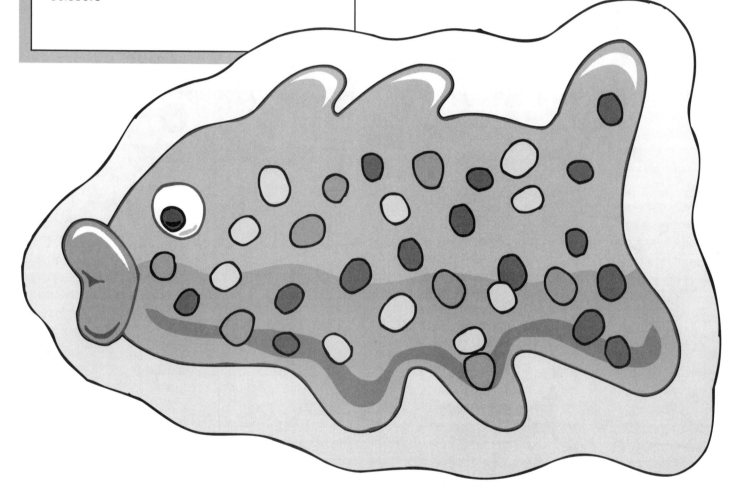

**Steps:**

1. Using a pen, draw the outline of a desired design on the plastic. (If desired, set the plastic atop a coloring-book design, and trace it with the pen.)
2. Fill in the design with various colors of fabric paint. Allow the paint to dry according to the directions.
3. Cut out the design, leaving a small edge of clear plastic around the painted area.
4. Wet the back of the plastic design and press it onto a window.

*Tina Merdinyan—Gr. 2, Kimball Elementary, Seattle, WA*

# Green-Haired Martian

**Materials for one Martian:**

| | |
|---|---|
| clear plastic cup | foil |
| construction-paper scraps | potting soil |
| scissors | grass seed |
| markers | water |
| textured items (such as buttons, | glue |
|   dry cereal, or paper cutouts) | |
| hole puncher | |
| 2 pipe cleaners | |
| four 1 1/2" squares of construction paper | |

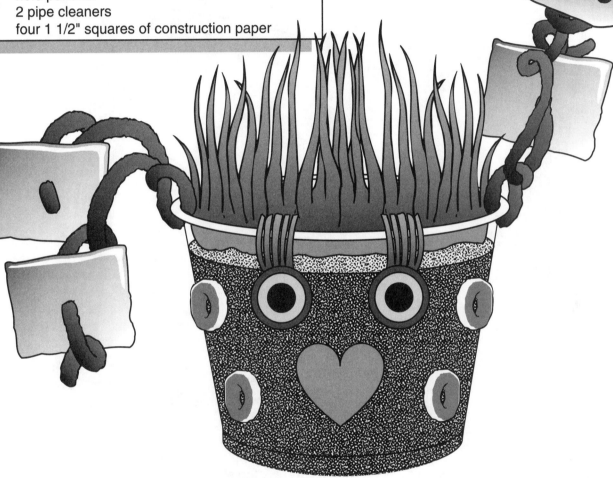

**Steps:**

1. Using construction-paper scraps, scissors, markers, various textured items, and glue, decorate the outside of the plastic cup to make an unusual face.
2. Using a hole puncher, punch a hole on either side of the cup near the top.
3. Insert the pipe cleaners through the holes and twist to secure them to the cup. Shape the pipe cleaners into desired positions for antennae.
4. Wrap 1 1/2-inch squares of construction paper with foil.
5. Poke a small hole in the center of each square. Slide the squares onto the ends of the pipe cleaners.
6. Fill the cup with potting soil. Plant grass seed in the soil.
7. Water the seeds slightly and place the cup in sunlight.
8. Water the Martian occasionally and watch him grow green hair!

*Jenny Eickhorst—Grs. 1–3, Blackhawk Christian School, Fort Wayne, IN*

# amped Apple Pictures

**Materials for one project:**

1 piece of 9" x 12" white construction paper
1 piece of 12" x 18" red or green construction
  paper
black India ink or diluted tempera paint
paintbrush (optional: if black paint is used)
red and green tempera paint
apple                          3 paper towels
paring knife                   drinking straw
sponge pieces                  glue

**Steps:**

1. In various places on the piece of white construction paper, drop five to six drops of black ink or diluted tempera paint.

2. Blow through the straw to spread the ink or paint on the paper to make branches. Add more drops of ink if needed. Allow the paint to dry.

3. Make a tempera-paint stamp pad by stacking three paper towels and pouring red tempera paint atop the towels. (Do not dilute the paint.) Allow the paint ample time to soak into the towels.

4. Cut an apple in half with the paring knife. (This step should be done by an adult.) Press half of the apple into the tempera-paint stamp pad and make apple prints on the white construction paper. Allow the apple prints to dry.

5. Dip the sponge pieces into green tempera paint and gently press them on the picture to make leaves. Let the paint dry.

6. Mount the project onto the piece of red or green construction paper.

Display these delightful pictures on a bulletin board entitled "The Apples Of Our Eyes."

*Lynda L. Neuroth—Learning Specialist,*
*Johnson Elementary, Livonia, MI*

# Hot Air Balloon

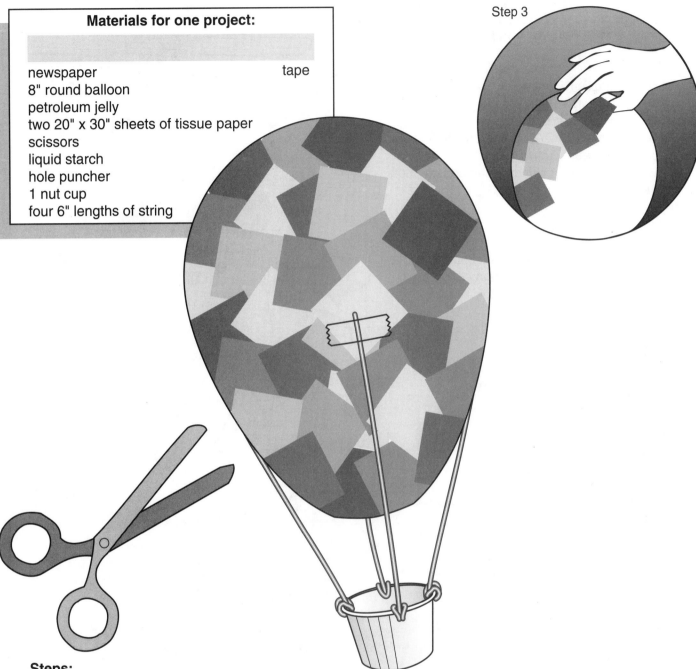

**Materials for one project:**

newspaper
8" round balloon
petroleum jelly
two 20" x 30" sheets of tissue paper
scissors
liquid starch
hole puncher
1 nut cup
four 6" lengths of string

tape

Step 3

**Steps:**

1. Spread newspaper atop your work surface before beginning this project.
2. Blow up the balloon and grease its surface with petroleum jelly.
3. Cut tissue paper into one-inch squares. One at a time, immerse the tissue-paper squares in liquid starch and attach them to the surface of the balloon. Slightly overlap the squares to cover the balloon completely. (Step 3) Continue in this manner until the balloon has been covered with two or three layers of tissue paper. Allow the balloon to dry for approximately two days.
4. When the balloon is dry, cut a two-inch hole in the bottom and remove the balloon. (If the balloon is not already deflated, use a pin to puncture it.) Set the tissue-paper balloon aside.
5. Using a hole puncher, punch four holes along the rim of a nut cup. Tie one end of a six-inch length of string through each hole.
6. To suspend the basket below the balloon, tape each piece of string to the side of the balloon.

*Gail Rothschiller—Gr. 4, Robert Miller School, Bismarck, ND*

# Frogs And Toads Together

**Step 2**

**fold**

**Step 3**

## Materials for one project:

1 small, plastic Dixie cup
crayons (brown and green)
arm and leg patterns below
1" x 6" strip of brown or green construction paper (folded in half)
1 ½" x 6" strip of brown or green construction paper (folded in half)
scissors
glue
two 2" squares of white construction paper
two 1 ½" squares of black construction paper
4 ½" x 6" piece of green construction paper
2" x 3" rectangle of yellow, pink, or white construction paper

**Patterns**

**arm pattern**

**leg pattern**

## Steps:

1. Using a crayon, color the outside and bottom of the cup brown for a toad or green for a frog.
2. Using the patterns shown, trace the arm onto a folded 1" x 6" strip of construction paper. Trace the leg onto a folded strip of 1 ½" x 6" construction paper. Cut out the resulting outlines. (Step 2) Open the folded outlines to reveal both arms and legs.
3. Turn the cup upside down and glue the legs to the back near the bottom of the cup. Glue the arms to the back of the cup above the legs. (Step 3)
4. Cut a circle from each of the white and black squares of construction paper for the eyes.

5. Glue each black circle atop a white circle. Attach the white circles to the front of the cup.
6. Cut a mouth from a scrap of black construction paper and glue it on.
7. Cut a lily pad shape from the green construction paper.
8. Put a trail of glue around the lip of the cup and glue it to the lily pad.
9. From yellow, pink, or white paper, cut a lily shape and glue the center of the flower to the lily pad. Bend the petals upward.

*Clealyn B. Wilson—Gr. 1, East Dover Elementary, Dover, DE*

# Puffy Panda

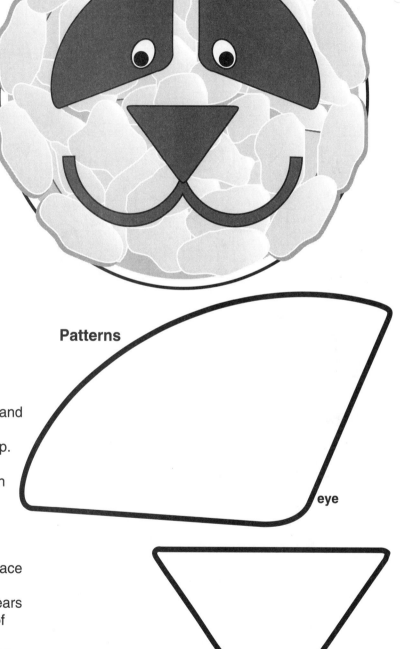

## Materials for one panda:

eye and nose patterns below
pencil
black construction paper
scissors
10 ¼" three-section Styrofoam plate
glue
pair of wiggle eyes
white cotton

Step 3

Step 4

Step 5

**Patterns**

eye

nose

## Steps:

1. Using the patterns for tracers, cut eyes and a nose from black construction paper.
2. Position the plate facedown on a tabletop.
3. Glue the construction-paper eyes to the small sections of the plate (Step 3). Then glue a wiggle eye atop each section.
4. Glue the nose to the large section of the plate as shown (Step 4).
5. Cut mouth pieces from scraps of black construction paper and glue them into place below the nose (Step 5).
6. From black construction paper, cut two ears and glue the ears in place near the top of the plate.
7. Loosen the cotton by pulling it gently apart. Glue the cotton to the exposed surfaces of the plate.

*Clealyn B. Wilson—Gr. 1, East Dover Elementary, Dover, DE*

# Fluttering Trio

**Materials for one project:**

**butterfly pattern on page 133**

12" x 18" white construction paper
black marker
crayons or oil pastels
12" x 18" construction paper
  (various colors)
scissors
pipe cleaner
stapler

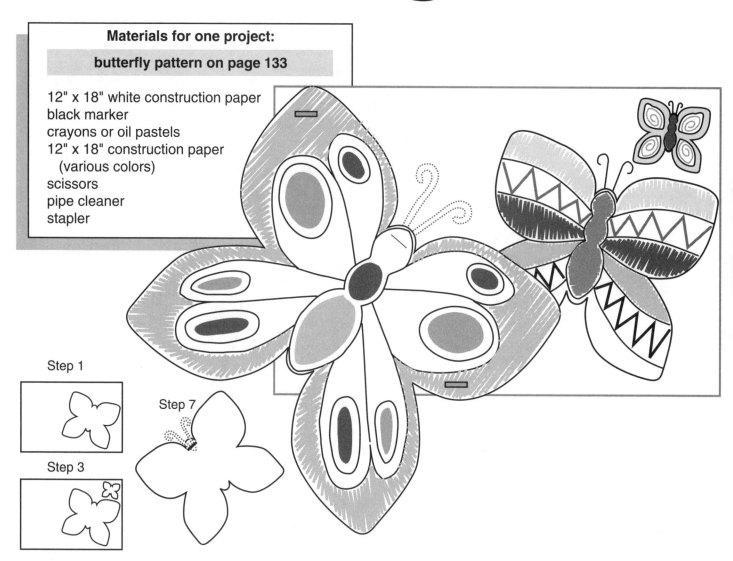

Step 1

Step 3

Step 7

## Steps:

(Use the pattern on page 133 for the medium-size butterfly. Then use a copying machine to enlarge the butterfly pattern for the large butterfly.)

1. With black marker, trace the medium-size pattern onto a piece of white 12" x18" construction paper. (This butterfly should be off to one side as shown in Step 1.)
2. Using the black marker, make symmetrical designs on the butterfly. Color the butterfly using crayons or oil pastels.
3. Draw a smaller butterfly on the same paper with a black marker (Step 3). Add symmetrical designs and color to it.
4. Color around the two butterflies to make a sky background.

5. Using the black marker, trace the large butterfly pattern onto a 12" x 18" piece of colored construction paper.
6. Color and cut out the resulting butterfly outline.
7. Bend a five-inch length of pipe cleaner into a *V* shape; then staple it behind the large butterfly's head (Step 7). Bend the ends of the pipe cleaner to complete the antennae.
8. Staple the large butterfly to the paper with the smaller butterflies.

This project is a demonstration of symmetry and the illusion of depth.

*Yvonne Rosser—Art Teacher, The Barstow School, Kansas City, MO*

Use with "Fluttering Trio" on page 132, "Beautiful Butterfly" on page 138, and "Torn Paper Butterfly" on page 144.

**Pattern**

# Fire-Breathing Dragon

**Materials for one dragon:**

paper cup
scissors
tape
red crepe-paper streamers or metallic ribbon
craft stick
glue
2 green pom-poms
pair of wiggle eyes

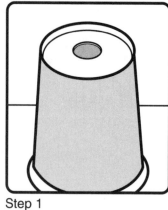

Step 1

Step 2

Step 3

**Steps:**

1. Cut a small hole in the bottom of the cup (Step 1).
2. Cut several streamers or pieces of ribbon and tape the ends inside the cup around the small hole (Step 2).
3. Glue a craft stick to the bottom of the cup as shown (Step 3). Allow the glue to dry.
4. Attach two pom-poms near the base of the cup. Glue a wiggle eye on each pom-pom.
5. To make the dragon breathe fire, hold onto the craft stick and blow through the hole in the base of the cup.

*Kimberle S. Byrd—Preschool, Mayflower Preschool, Grand Rapids, MI*

134

# Big-Nosed Clown

## Materials for one clown:

construction paper
tagboard (optional)
pencil
scissors
paper plate
glue
crayons or markers
balloon

Step 6

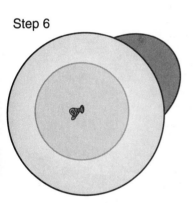

**Steps:**
*(Prior to doing this art project, make a clown hat pattern from a seven-inch square of construction paper or tagboard.)*

1. Trace the hat pattern onto construction paper.
2. Cut out and glue the clown hat to the paper plate.
3. Using crayons or markers, decorate the clown hat. Draw eyes and a mouth on the paper plate, leaving a space for the clown's nose.
4. Poke a small hole in the paper plate for the nose.
5. Blow up a balloon and knot the end. (This step should be done for each child by the teacher.)
6. Gently push the knot of the balloon through the front of the hole to give your clown a big balloon nose (Step 6).

*Joan A. Koszalka—Special Education,
Canaan Elementary, Patchogue, NY*

135

# Raggedy Ann And Andy

## Materials for one project:

4" white tagboard circle
5" lengths of red yarn
construction-paper scraps (red and black)
black marker or crayon
scissors
hole puncher
glue

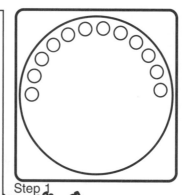
Step 1

Step 2

## Steps:

1. Using the hole puncher, punch holes half-way around the circle's edge (Step 1).
2. Thread two lengths of yarn through each hole for hair and knot the yarn as shown (Step 2).
3. From construction-paper scraps, cut black circle eyes, a red triangle nose, and red circle cheeks. Glue the facial features to the circle.
4. Use the black marker to draw additional facial features.

If desired, loop a long length of yarn through one of the holes and suspend your students' Raggedy Anns and Andys from the ceiling.

*Becky Honaker—Gr. K, New Richmond Elementary, New Richmond, OH*

136

# Stand-Up Penguin

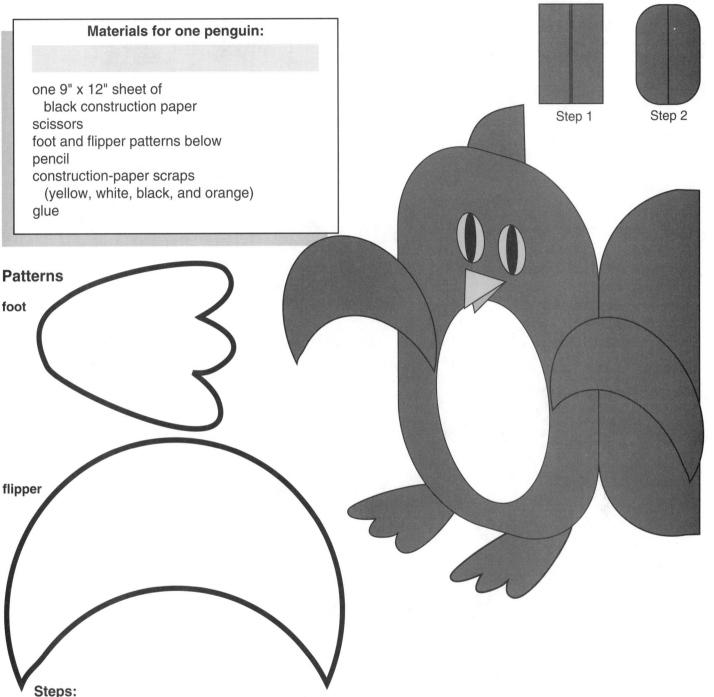

Step 1

Step 2

**Materials for one penguin:**

one 9" x 12" sheet of
  black construction paper
scissors
foot and flipper patterns below
pencil
construction-paper scraps
  (yellow, white, black, and orange)
glue

**Patterns**

foot

flipper

**Steps:**

1. Position the 9" x 12" sheet of black construction paper horizontally on a tabletop. Fold in and crease the narrow ends so that they meet in the center of the paper (Step 1).
2. Cut off the corners of the paper at the folds in a rounded fashion to form an oval for the penguin's body (Step 2).
3. Using the tracers, cut two black feet and two black flippers. Glue these pieces in place.
4. Cut a white oval from construction paper and glue it to the front of the penguin's body.
5. Cut eyes from yellow construction paper and a beak from orange construction paper. Glue these pieces in place on the penguin's face.
6. To make the penguin stand up, bend its feet forward at the base of its body. Then open the folded flaps until the body balances against the flaps.

*Pam Hawkins—Pre-K, Lawrenceville, GA*

137

# Beautiful Butterfly

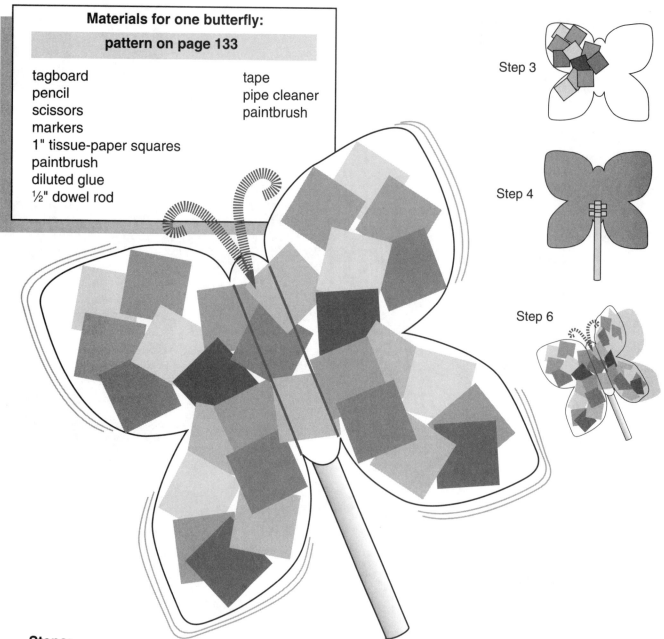

**Materials for one butterfly:**

**pattern on page 133**

tagboard
pencil
scissors
markers
1" tissue-paper squares
paintbrush
diluted glue
½" dowel rod

tape
pipe cleaner
paintbrush

Step 3

Step 4

Step 6

## Steps:

1. Using the pattern on page 133, trace or duplicate a butterfly on tagboard. Cut on the resulting outline.
2. Color one side of the butterfly with markers.
3. On the opposite side of the butterfly, brush diluted glue atop varied colors of tissue-paper squares to cover the surface. Allow the glue to dry.
4. Tape the end of the dowel rod to the base of the butterfly as shown in Step 4.
5. Curl the ends of a pipe cleaner, bend it, and tape it to the butterfly's head for antennae.
6. To create wings that flap, make a fold at the base of each wing as indicated in Step 6.

Have each child hold onto the dowel rod and fly his butterfly around the room!

*Ann Marie Guinn—Gr. K, Harmony-Leland School, Mableton, GA*

# Dazzling Dragonfly

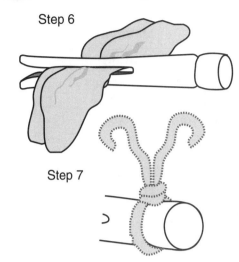

Step 6

Step 7

**Materials for one dragonfly:**

round-head clothespin
paint
paintbrush
glitter
glue
pair of tiny wiggle eyes
dragonfly wing pattern below
tissue paper (two or more colors)

scissors
pipe cleaner

**pattern**

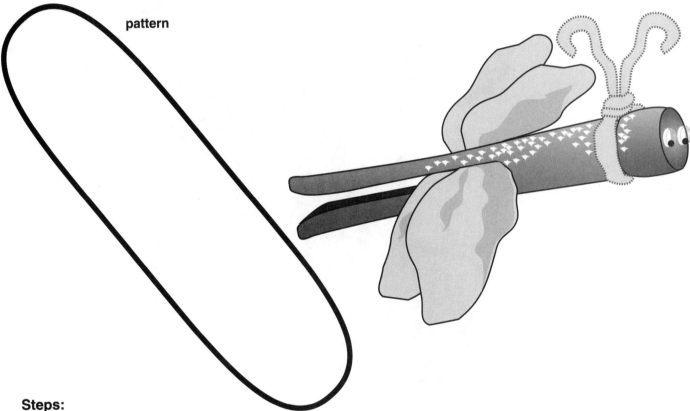

**Steps:**

1. Paint the clothespin and sprinkle it with glitter while the paint is still wet.
2. Allow the paint to dry.
3. Glue the pair of wiggle eyes to the head of the clothespin.
4. Using the pattern shown, cut a pair of wings from each of two colors of tissue paper.
5. Crumple the wings to add stiffness.
6. Glue the tissue-paper wings inside the clothespin as indicated in the diagram (Step 6).
7. Cut a five-inch piece of pipe cleaner. Wrap the pipe cleaner around the dragonfly's head for antennas; twist to secure it. (Step 7). Bend each end of the pipe cleaner.

Display your dragonflies by attaching lengths of thread to suspend them.

*Sherry Fenton—Gr. 2, Ernest Stapleton Elementary, Albuquerque, NM*

# offee Grounds Teddy Bear

| Materials for one bear: |
| --- |
| **pattern on page 123** |

tagboard
pencil
scissors
glue
cotton swab
used coffee grounds, dried
pair of wiggle eyes
2 buttons
length of ribbon

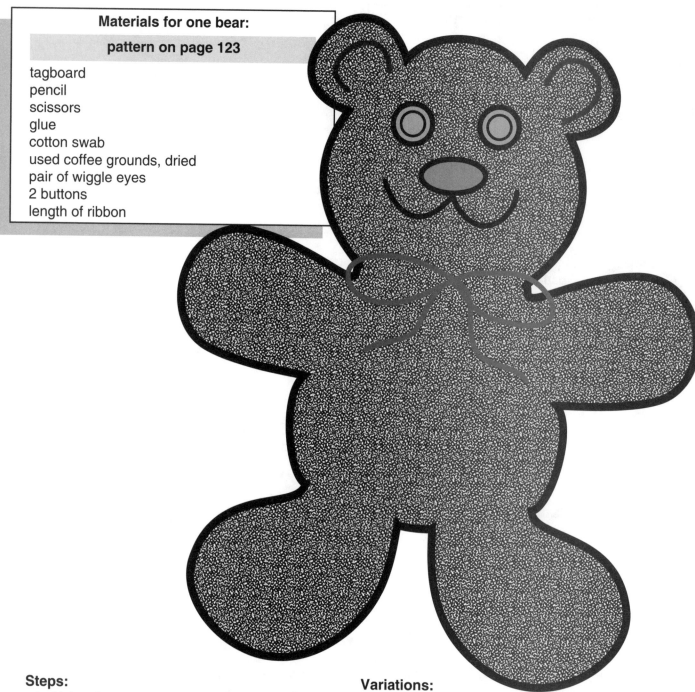

**Steps:**

1. Using the tracer on page 123, trace the bear outline on tagboard and cut it out.
2. Use a cotton swab to fill in the outline with a coat of glue.
3. Sprinkle a generous amount of coffee grounds onto the glue. Shake off the excess coffee grounds and let the glue dry overnight.
4. Decorate the bear by attaching wiggle eyes, buttons, and ribbon tied in a bow.

**Variations:**

—Fill a snowman outline with salt.
—Fill a dog outline with ground cinnamon.
—Fill an owl outline with sunflower seeds.
—Fill a giraffe outline with pieces of colored egg shells.

*Deborah Pruett—Preschool, Mt. Pleasant School, Terre Haute, IN*

# Field Trip T-Shirts

**Materials for one shirt:**

white T-shirt
fabric marker
cardboard
fabric dye (Use a brand such as Tulip Dye.
   It will be permanent on the shirt, but not on
   skin if it's wiped off while it is wet.)
paint trays
paper towels

Jackson Crane
Webster Elementary
Mrs. Ensley

**Steps:**

1. Using a fabric marker, write the names of the child, the teacher, and the school in large letters on the front of the shirt.
2. Before painting, place a piece of cardboard inside the shirt to prevent the paint from leaking through.
3. Make handprints on the front of the shirt with various colors of fabric dye. Clean students' hands with paper towels before changing colors.
4. Set the shirt aside to dry thoroughly.

*Donna Ferraro—Gr. K, St. Joseph's School, Penfield, NY*

# Pressed Flower Picture

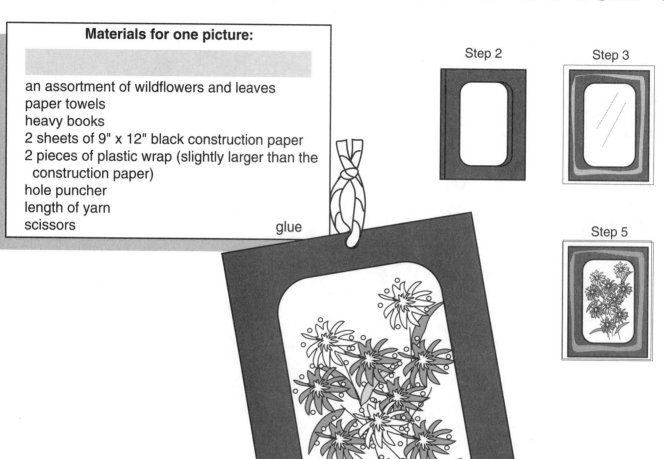

**Materials for one picture:**

an assortment of wildflowers and leaves
paper towels
heavy books
2 sheets of 9" x 12" black construction paper
2 pieces of plastic wrap (slightly larger than the
   construction paper)
hole puncher
length of yarn
scissors                                          glue

Step 2

Step 3

Step 5

**Steps:**

1. Collect a variety of wildflowers and leaves. Press them between pieces of paper towels placed inside heavy books. Press the flowers for two to three weeks to dry them.

2. Stack the two sheets of construction paper and align the edges. Cut a large oval in the middle of both sheets of paper, forming a window for the frame. (Step 2)

3. Position one of the frame pieces on a tabletop. Set the other frame piece aside. Squeeze a trail of glue along the edge of the frame. Lay one piece of plastic wrap atop the glue and press it gently in place. (Step 3)

4. Place an assortment of pressed flowers and leaves atop the plastic wrap in a desired arrangement.

5. Squeeze a trail of glue along the edge of the frame atop the plastic. Squeeze a few small drops of glue on the pressed flowers. Then carefully place the other piece of plastic wrap atop the flowers and press down gently on the glued areas. (Step 5)

6. Glue the other frame piece atop the arrangement, aligning the outer edges of the frame. Press the finished frame between two heavy books to set the glue.

7. Trim the excess plastic from the edges of the frame.

8. Using a hole puncher, punch a hole in the top of the frame. Attach a length of yarn and hang the frame in a window.

*Jane Ransdell—Grs. K–2, Platte Valley District 8, North Platte, NE*

# I Like Me!

## Materials for one project:

paper grocery bag
wrapping paper
two 9" x 3" strips of construction paper
two 12" x 4" strips of construction paper
construction paper (appropriate colors for hands,
   shoes, and hair)
crayons and markers
sturdy 9" paper plate
fabric trims (such as ricrac, lace, and ribbon)

pencil
glue
yarn
stapler
newspaper
tape
scissors
paintbrush
tempera paints

Step 1

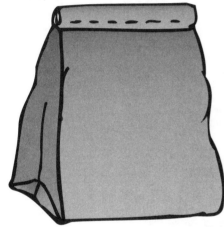

**Steps:**

1. Fill a grocery bag with crumpled newspaper
   and staple the bag closed (Step 1).
2. Paint the outside of the bag, or wrap the bag
   in brightly colored wrapping paper and cut
   and tape it to form a shirt or blouse.
3. For arms staple a 9" x 3" construction-paper
   strip near the top of each side of the bag.
4. Staple two 12" x 4" strips of construction
   paper near the bottom of the bag for legs.
5. Trace around your shoes and hands on
   construction paper, and cut on the resulting
   outlines. Decorate the shoes and hands,
   and glue them in place.

6. Decorate the paper plate to look like you
   with facial features and hair made from
   markers, crayons, yarn, construction paper,
   and other available materials.
7. Staple the plate to the top of the bag.
8. Use fabric trims to add details to the clothes,
   the shoes, or the hair.

This is a great self-esteem project to accompany
the book *I Like Me!* by Nancy Carlson.

*Carol Komperda—Gr. K, Albany Avenue School,*
*North Massapequa, NY*

# Torn Paper Butterfly

**Steps:**

1. Trace or duplicate the butterfly pattern on page 133 onto construction paper, and cut on the resulting outline.
2. Tear one-inch pieces from brightly colored magazine pictures.
3. Glue the torn pieces in collage fashion to cover the entire butterfly.
4. Cut antennae from black construction paper and glue them to the back of the butterfly's head.

Suspend the butterflies from a length of yarn for a decorative display.

*Laura M. Morrison—Gr. 3, Manassas Park Elementary, Manassas Park, VA*

# Scratchboard Art

**Materials for one scratchboard:**

white tagboard
crayons
black tempera paint
paper clip
paintbrush

Step 2

**Steps:**

1. Color the entire piece of tagboard heavily with various colors of crayons.
2. Brush black tempera paint over the colored surface as shown in Step 2. (Two to three coats of paint will be needed.)
3. Allow the tagboard to dry for one day.
4. Use the paper clip to scratch into the black paint, creating a brightly colored design.

*Debra Lynn Dechaine, Plainville, CT*

# Genie In A Bottle

**Materials for one project:**

construction paper
pencil
scissors
fabric scraps
fabric trims (such as ribbon, ricrac, and lace)
glitter
glue
2-liter, clear plastic bottle
X-acto knife

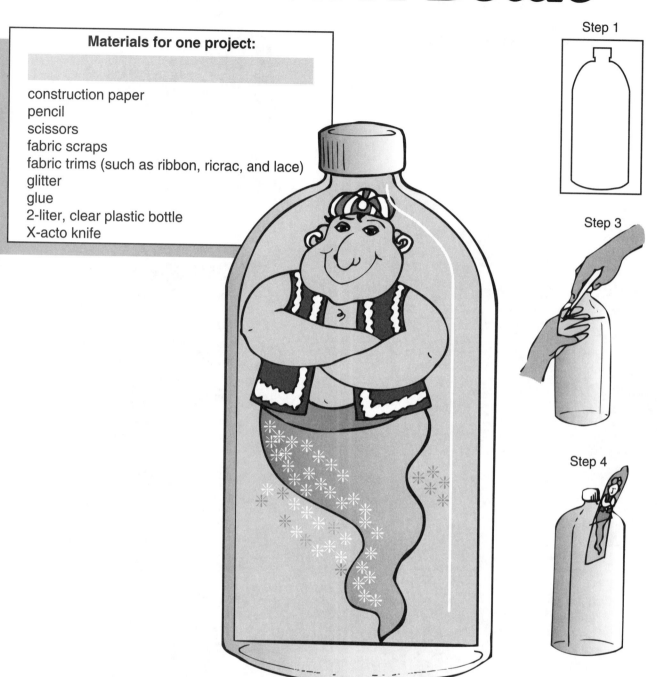

Step 1

Step 3

Step 4

## Steps:

*(Prior to this art project, make a bottle pattern that is slightly smaller than your plastic bottle.)*

1. Trace the bottle pattern onto construction paper and cut out the resulting outline (Step 1).
2. Draw a genie on the bottle cutout and decorate his clothing with fabric scraps, construction paper, fabric trims, and glitter. Let it dry and shake off any excess glitter.

3. Near the top of the plastic bottle, cut a slit that is the width of the bottle cutout (Step 3). (This should be done by an adult using an X-acto knife.)
4. Slip the genie through the hole to display him in the bottle (Step 4).

This is a great project to make after reading one of the Aladdin stories.

*Cecile Shetler—Gr. 3, Louisiana State University Lab School, Baton Rouge, LA*

# Shoot-A-Shirt

**Materials for one shirt:**

white T-shirt
flat gift box
squirt gun
fabric dye or fabric paint
  (that can be diluted)
plastic jewels
sequins
fabric glue
plastic tarp

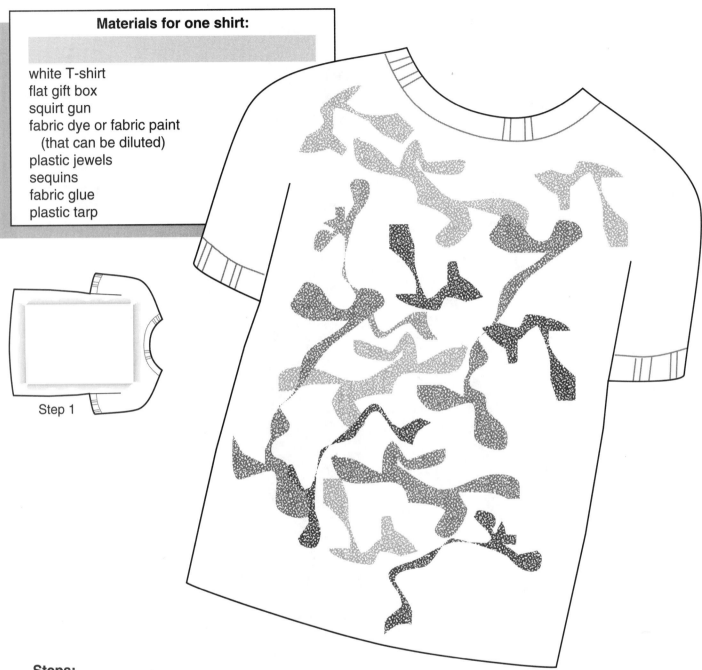

Step 1

**Steps:**

1. Stretch the  T-shirt over the flat gift box. (Step 1)
2. Fill the squirt gun with fabric dye or diluted fabric paint (one part paint to three parts water).

3. Before continuing this project, spread a tarp on the floor or take the materials outside. Prop up the box with the T-shirt. Then, using the squirt gun, shoot the paint at the T-shirt to create the desired markings. Allow the shirt to dry.
4. Use fabric glue to attach sequins and plastic jewels in various places on the shirt. Let the glue dry according to the directions.

*Rosemary Bonelli—Gr. Pre-K, Building Blocks School, Commack, NY*

# Tube People

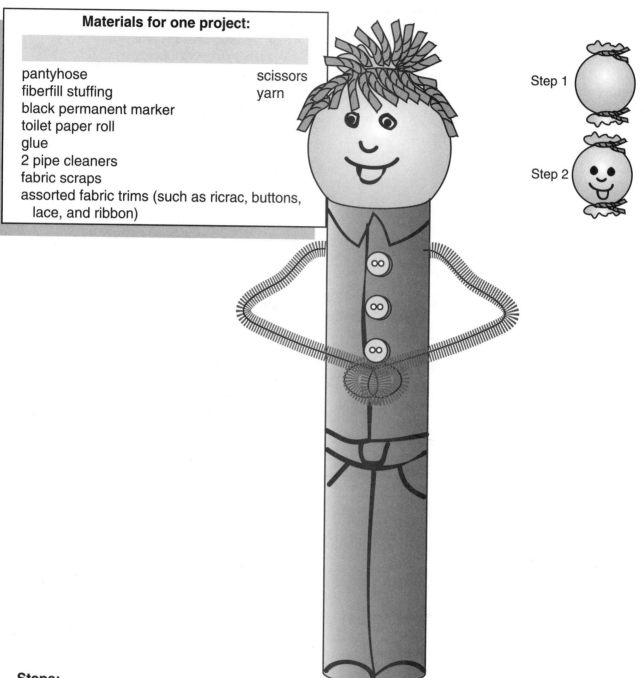

**Materials for one project:**

pantyhose          scissors
fiberfill stuffing     yarn
black permanent marker
toilet paper roll
glue
2 pipe cleaners
fabric scraps
assorted fabric trims (such as ricrac, buttons,
    lace, and ribbon)

Step 1

Step 2

**Steps:**

1. To make the tube person's head, stuff a section of pantyhose with fiberfill stuffing large enough to fit atop the toilet paper roll. Tie a knot above and below the fiberfill, and cut off the excess material. (Step 1)

2. Position the head so that the knots are on the top and bottom. Then, using the black marker, draw a face on the head. (Step 2)

3. Glue the head to the top of the toilet paper roll.

4. Poke a hole in either side of the tube. Insert a pipe cleaner in each hole. Then decorate the toilet paper roll to look like clothing using fabric scraps, fabric trims, scissors, and glue.

5. Glue lengths of yarn onto the head for hair.

*Kelly Kingsley—Gr. 5, Wake Robin School, Bellevue, NE*

# Pinecone Bee

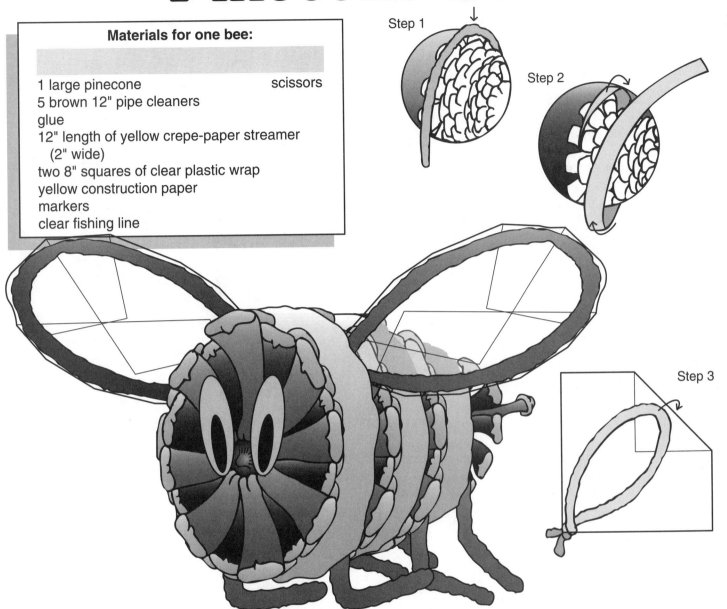

**Materials for one bee:**

1 large pinecone          scissors
5 brown 12" pipe cleaners
glue
12" length of yellow crepe-paper streamer
  (2" wide)
two 8" squares of clear plastic wrap
yellow construction paper
markers
clear fishing line

Step 1

Step 2

Step 3

## Steps:

1. To attach legs to the bee's body, bend each of three pipe cleaners around the front, middle, and back of the cone. Pull the middle of each pipe cleaner between the pinecone scales. Apply glue to secure the legs. (Step 1)
2. Tuck one end of the yellow streamer between the scales at the front of the cone. Wrap the streamer around the cone to make stripes as shown in Step 2. Use small amounts of glue to secure the ends of the streamer.
3. Form two ovals from the remaining pipe cleaners. Twist the ends of each pipe cleaner together to close the shape. Wrap each oval with a square of plastic wrap. (Step 3)

4. Push the ends of the ovals between the scales on either side of the pinecone to make wings. Glue the wings in place and allow the glue to dry.
5. From yellow construction paper, cut two circles for eyes. Embellish the eyes with markers as desired and glue them to the front of the bee.
6. Attach a length of clear fishing line and suspend your bee among a garden of paper flowers.

*Lois Myers—Gr. 1, Hillcrest Christian School, Bethel Park, PA*

# Salt Box Bird

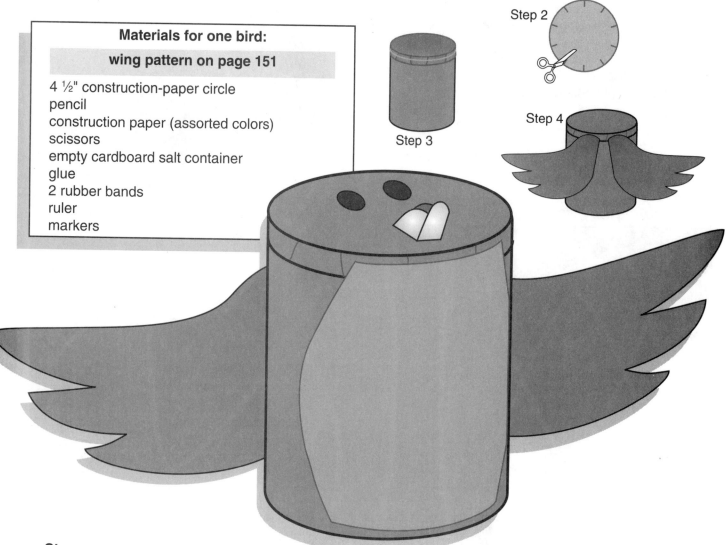

Step 2

Step 3

Step 4

**Materials for one bird:**

**wing pattern on page 151**

4 ½" construction-paper circle
pencil
construction paper (assorted colors)
scissors
empty cardboard salt container
glue
2 rubber bands
ruler
markers

## Steps:

*(Prior to this activity, make a 4 ½-inch contruction-paper circle for a tracer.)*

1. Using the tracer, cut two 4 ½-inch circles from one color of construction paper.
2. Cut approximately ten ½-inch slits around the outer edge of each circle (Step 2).
3. Spread a coat of glue atop the salt container, avoiding the metal spout area. Press one circle atop the glue. Fold down the tabs between the slits along the container's edges and glue them to the side of the container. Use a rubber band to hold the tabs in place while the glue dries. Repeat this procedure for the bottom of the container (Step 3). Remove the rubber bands when the glue is dry.
4. With adult assistance, cut away the construction paper atop the container to expose the metal spout. Open the spout to form a beak.

5. Using the same color of construction paper, cut a 10 ½" x 5 ¼" strip. Spread a coat of glue on one side of the strip and wrap the paper around the container to cover the bird's body.
6. Using the patterns on page 151, trace two wings on the same or a contrasting color of construction paper. Cut on the resulting outlines.
7. Glue the straight edges of the wings to the body of the bird as shown.
8. Use markers and various colors of construction paper to add details—such as eyes, stripes, and colored breast feathers—to the bird.

*Trudi Campbell—Gr. 2, Central Elementary, Bemidji, MN*